LIBRARY 3.0
An Innovative Tool in Knowledge Epoch

LIBRARY 3.0
An Innovative Tool in Knowledge Epoch

By
Dr. Nasirudheen. T
(Dr.) Ravi Kumar Merugu

Foreword
Dr. A. Kumaraswamy
DEAN, Defence Institute of Advanced Technology, Pune

Ess Ess Publications
New Delhi

LIBRARY 3.0 : An Innovative Tool in Knowledge Epoch

ISBN : 978-93-87698-21-5

First Published 2019

Published by:
Ess Ess Publications
4831/24, Ansari Road,
Darya Ganj,
New Delhi-110 002.
INDIA
Phones: 23260807, 41563444
Fax: 41563334
E-mail: info@essessreference.com
www.essessreference.com

Cover Design by *Patch Creative Unit*

Printed and bound in India

Contents

Dr. A. Kumaraswamy
Dean (Technology),
Professor & Head, Mechanical Engineering and
Chairman, Doctoral Research Committee,
Defence Institute of Advanced Technology (DU),Pune
(An autonomous institute funded by Department of Defence R&D,
Ministry of Defence, Government of India)

FOREWORD

Libraries play an **important** role in research and education. **Digital library** provides access to many of the knowledge networks around the world, which is a necessary component of any research experience. *Repositories* provide a method of sharing content for different viewers. Outcome from the research such as publications and data are not only used by other researchers but are also *important* resources for students. Research outputs as well as learning objects are *important* parts of the learning lifecycle.

Modern libraries are complex systems that consist of many systems and subsystems that include acquisition of materials, cataloging and classification, circulation and interlibrary loan, serials management and reference services. The most important function, however, has been providing service to the users. For centuries, librarians have managed warehouses of documents by acquiring, cataloging and classifying books, journals and other materials and circulating them to their clients. Computer and communication technologies have facilitated the new breed of information professionals to select, organize, retrieve, and transfer (SORT) the actual information effectively and efficiently to the users.

Needless to mention that, current day library professionals must be equipped with the skill set in demand in emerging technological developments for providing quality and efficient service to the customers. Especially, how to implement digital libraries, institutional repositories and library automation using open source software to reduce the financial burden on the organizations/institutions whether it is government or private.

It gives me immense pleasure to present the book on '*LIBRARY 3.0 - An Innovative Tool in Knowledge Epoch*' written by Dr.Nasirudheen T, Junior Librarian, University of Calicut, Kerala and Mr. Ravi Kumar Merugu, PhD Scholar & Senior Library & Information Assistant in Sardar Vallabhbhai Patel National Police Academy, Hyderabad, Telangana. The authors have explained various important aspects viz. necessity of library app, installation of drupal software, evolution of Library 3.0, virtual library services, features of NewGenlib software, knowledge management, ICT initiations, institutional repositories, copy right issues, measurement of service quality with LIBQUAL+ tool two features in one software, English language skills, data mining & Artificial intelligence in libraries etc covered in six chapters in a very lucid manner.

I am pretty confident that, the efforts of the authors to impart technical knowledge will be well received by library professionals, students, research scholars and computer techies in library 3.0. I wish the authors all the best in their future endeavors.

Dr. A. Kumarswamy

Preface

The invention of wheel and ICT revolution are the two remarkable achievements in the history of mankind. The former one helped to move from one place to another place and to travel throughout the world, where as the latter one helped to bring the whole world into our hands. Information and Communication Technology is growing beyond our imagination. It has influenced each and every sphere of human life.

Presently web technology has been reached its third version, viz web 3.0 and it is also known as semantic web. It is the dynamic version of the web and Web 3.0 represents an evolutionary shift in how people interact with the web, and vice versa. The features of web 3.0 are artificial Intelligence, automated reasoning, cognitive architecture, composite applications, distributed computing, knowledge representation, ontology (computer service), recombinant text, scalable vector graphics etc.

Library 3.0 is the result of integration of web 3.0 technologies into the Library and Information services. It refers to libraries using technologies such as the semantic web, cloud computing, mobile devices and re-envisioning our use of established technologies such as federated search to facilitate user-generated content and collaboration to promote and make library collections accessible.

It has been include here 16 papers on different areas of web 3.0 and library 3.0 and has broadly categorised as - Web 3.0 & Library 3.0 Open source Library software, Knowledge Management & Data mining, Artificial Intelligence, ICT initiatives & repositories Legal, Psychological & Linguistic issues in ICT. We the editors would like to submit this valuable work to the whole LIS community with great pleasure and gratitude.

— Editors

Acknowledgement

First of all we express our utmost gratitude to almighty God, for his grace, strength and patience poured upon me throughout this work.

We express our deep gratitude to Shri. Dr. K.P.AIlyas, IPS, Assistant Director (I/c Library), SVP National Police Academy for his great support, motivation and encouragement.Our Special Thanks to Shri.PrakashWalke (LIO), Shri.P.Pradeep (ALIO), Shri.K.Nirmal Kumar (SLIA), Shri.C.N.Hemanth (SLIA) and all other Library staff of SVP National Police Academy who always guiding and supporting our in all aspects.

We gratified to Anil Kumar, Lecturer in Library Science, CKM Arts & Science College, Warangal, BandiYugandhar, Lecturer in Library Science, Govt,Degree College, Mulugu, Warangal &all our friends and well-wishers who are always encouraging and supporting me in all our endeavors.

We must thank to parents of Mr. Ravikumar Merugu (Chandraiah&Venkatamma), bothers & their family members for their love, support and tolerance in all facets. Also, our heartfelt thanks to my better-off of Mr. Ravikumar Merugu (Priyanka) for her bountiful cooperation and moral support rendered, and lovely sons Sai Sankeerth and Sai Puneeth for their patience throughout long-term period of the preparation of this book.

We have special thanks to parents of Dr. Nasirudheen. T (Moidu Master & Fathima), his beloved wife Ahsanath, Henna (daughter)Hanaf (son) and all other friends and family members for their mental support and patience.

We are also obliged to all the contributors who supported us with their manuscripts and showed their trust on us; special thanks to Ess Ess Publications, New Delhi for the receiving of our proposal for publication of this great productivity in shortest period.

— **Editors**

Contributors

1. Dr. Nasiruddeen.T
Junior Librarian, University of Calicut, Thrissur, Calicut Road, Thenhipalam , Kerala

2. (Dr.) Ravi Kumar Merugu
Senior Library & Information Assisitant, Sardar Vallabhbhai Patel National Police Academy, Hyderabad, Telangana & Research Scholar.

3. A. Durga Prasad
Assistant Professor, Library Science, Nagarjuna Govt. College, (Autonomous) Nalgonda, Telengana

4. Gatla Krishna Reddy
Librarian, S.K.N.R Govt. Arts & Science College, Jagtial, Telangana

5. Muduganti Deepthi Reddy
Librarian, Alphores Womens Degree & P.G. College, Karimnagar, Telangana

6. Dodla Rajeshwar
Librarian, CMR Engineering College, Hyderabad, Telangana

7. Dr. Akhtar Hussain
Assistant Librarian, NIEPID Regional Centre, Gautambudh Nagar, Noida

8. Sreelatha K
Professional Assistant, CHMK Library, University of Calicut

9. Rajib Kalita
Research Scholar, Department of Library & Information Science, Gauhati University, Assam

10. Dr. Mehaboobullah.K
Reference Assistant, University of Kerala, Thiruvananthapuram. Kerala.

11. Kura Srinivas
Senior Librarian, Sri Venkateshwara Engineering College, Suryapet, Telangana

12. Simhachalam Terli
Assistant Librarian, Dr. B. R. Ambedkar Central Library, Adikavi Nannaya University, Rajamahendravaram, Andhra Pradesh

13. Ramesh Randhi
Assistant Professor,
Department of Library Science,
RGUKT, (IIIT),Srikulam,
Andhra Pradesh

14. Veerender Kumar, P
Assistant Professor in English, Sree Chaitanya Institute of Technological Sciences, Karimnagar, Telangana & Research Scholar (PT), Department of English, Kakatiya University, Warangal, Telangana

PART-I

Web 3.0 & Library 3.0

1

Evolution of Web to Web 3.0 and Library to Library 3.0

*Dr. Nasirudheen.T**

1. INTRODUCTION

Information and Communication Technology (ICT) has drastically revolutionized all spheres of human life. Library and Information service is one among the area, which absorbed and utilized the benefits of ICT from the very beginning itself. This field is traveling along the developments. The evolution of web from static to dynamic is treated as the starting of democratization. By the advent of web 3.0, by exploiting the benefits, library became library 3.0. and moving along with technologies.

2. EVOLUTION OF WEB

The World Wide Web is a system of interlinked hypertext document can be accessed with the support of Internet with a web browser. One can view web pages

* Junior Librarian, University of Calicut, Kerala.

that may contain text, image, videos, and other multimedia and navigate between them via hyper links. World wide web was invented by Tim Berners-Lee, a British computer scientist and former CERN employee in 1989.

2.1. Web 1.0

Web 1.0 is termed as the first generation of web starting from 1989 to 2005. It was defined as web of information connection. During this period, only one way interaction was possible through this set up. Interactions of users were hardly seen during this period. The role of the web was very passive in nature. During this period web was considered as an information space in which the items of interest referred to as resources are identified by global identifier called as Uniform Resources Identifiers (URLs).

Features

- They have read only content.
- Establish an on line presence and make their information available to anyone at any time.
- It includes static web pages and use basic Hypertext Mark-Up Language.

Limitations

- They have read only content. Establish an online presence and make their information available to anyone at any time. It includes static web pages and use basic Hypertext Mark-Up Language.
- The Web master is solely responsible for updating user and managing the content of website.
- Lack of Dynamic representation i.e., to acquire only static information, no web console were available to performing dynamic events.

2.2. Web 2.0

The evolution from web 1.0 to web 2.0 is occurred

due to the rapid growth of information technology. Web 2.0 is treated as the second generation of web which enabled interaction and it became dynamic. The former version of web was read only, where as the second version became read and write. In Web 2.0, the user can, not only receive information, but also contribute and modify the available content. Social networking sites such as Facebook, Orkut, LinkedIn are the prominent icons of web 2.0. Web 2.0 facilitates major properties like participatory, collaborative, and distributed practices which enable formal and in formal spheres of daily activities on going on web.

Tim O'Reilly defines web 2.0 on his website as follows "Web 2.0 is the business revolution in the computer industry caused by the move to the internet as platform, and an attempt to understand the rules for success on that new platform. Chief among those rules is this. Build applications that harness network effects to get better the more people use them".

2.2.1. Tools of web 2.0

There are many communities where people interact, share knowledge and learn. The important and most popular communities are:

2.2.1.1. Social Networks

Social networks sites (SNS) are web-based services that allow individuals to construct a public or semi- public profile within a bounded system, articulate a list of other users with whom they share a connection, and view and traverse their list of connections and those made by others within the system. The nature and nomenclature of these connections may vary from site to site. Facebook and twitter are predominant general social networking sites, while LinkedIn and Eacademy are professional social networks. Whatsapp is an exclusive social networking sites for smart phones.

2.2.1.2. Blogs

Blog is type of website maintained by an individual, wherein an individual can share thoughts, photos and videos about events and some cases where other people can comment on it. It is also a shared online journal where people share their personal knowledge and experience on various issues. Almost all the blogs have comment feature-enabled. There are many websites like, eblogger, blogger and google blog, etc which give platforms for bolgs.

2.2.1.3. RSS

RSS means – Really Simple Syndication. It is a family of web feed formats used to publish frequently updated works – such as blog entries, news headlines, audio, and video – in a standardized format. With this small RSS, the person can have updated real-time information.

2.2.1.4. Video / photo Sharing

YouTube is again the most popular website wherein people can share video, download videos and comment on them. People share knowledge and experience via YouTube. Flickr is a website that is popular for photo sharing service and also to comment on photos.

2.2.1.5. Wiki

Wiki is a website that allows the easy creation and editing of any number of interlinked web pages via a web browser using a simplified markup language. They are typically powered by wiki software and are often used to create collaborative websites, to power community websites, for personal note taking, in corporate intranets, and in knowledge management systems.

2.2.1.6. Podcast

Podcasts are digital media files which may be audio or video that can be downloaded through web by I-pod and I-pod like devices using Internet service. There are websites available like podcasting- tools.com which provide podcasting services.

2.2.1.7. Bookmarks

New web browsers have bookmarks options wherein users can bookmark their favorite websites so that it will be easy for them to access when necessary.

2.3. Web 3.0

Web 3.0 is a third generation of Internet-based Web services, which emphasize machine-facilitated understanding of information in order to provide a more productive and intuitive user experience. It is said that Web 3.0 is like a human being with practical knowledge. The term 'Web 3.0' was first coined by John Markoff of the New York Times in 2006, and first appeared significantly in early 2006 in a Blog article "Critical of Web 2.0 and associated technologies such as Ajax" written by Jeffrey Zeldman.

2.3.1. Web 3.0 Technologies

- Artificial Intelligence.
- Automated reasoning.
- Cognitive architecture.
- Composite applications.
- Distributed computing.
- Knowledge representation.
- Ontology (computer service).
- Recombinant text.
- Scalable vector graphics.
- Semantic Web.
- Semantic wiki, and
- Software agent

2.3.2. Characteristics of Web 3.0

- Saas Business Model.

- Open source software platform.
- Distributed Database or what called as ¯The World Wide Database .
- Web Personalization.
- Resource Pooling.
- Intelligent Web.

2.3.3. Structure of web 3.0

Compared to the web 1.0 and 2.0,. the basic structure of Web 3.0 is different . The basic structure is characterized by semiotics and semantics. Semantics refers to the study of meaning in communication, whereas, semiotics is the study of sign processes (semiosis), or signification and communication, signs and symbols, both individually and grouped into sign systems. It includes the study of how a meaning is constructed and understood. “Semantics can be very useful to the user as it helps him in arriving at the right answer for his query.

2.3.4. Advantages of web 3.0

1. Web 3.0 improves data management. management of data in websites is a complex process, as combining data from various structures requires knowledge of many applications and, in some cases, the computer may or may not be able to understand some data. in such cases, it becomes very difficult to link data for obtaining the required input. this problem can be resolved to some extent with the adoption of semantic web because it first describes the relationship between different sets of data which makes it easier for the computer to understand the relationship and integrates them easily for obtaining the desired output.
2. Web 3.0 supports accessibility of mobile internet globally. it is expected to play a very important role in enhancing the accessibility of the internet through mobile devices. web 3.0 is based on cascading style

sheet (css) standard, which helps in reducing the size of the page to less than 20kb.

3. Web 3.0 stimulates creativity and innovation. The main feature of web 3.0 is the flexibility of linking different databases. the information and knowledge datasets can be utilized equally by the systems, as well as human beings, thereby enhancing their efficiency. This encourages an innovation process which, in turn, helps in the generation of ideas and also in research & developments to create a new model.

4. Web 3.0 encourages factor of globalization Phenomena Web 3.0 aims at building and standardizing various data structures through a common programming language known as resource description framework (RDF). This is the standard model for exchanging data on the Web. RDF is written in XML, which facilitates easy exchange of information among different systems. This breaks the barriers of bandwidth, poor display of Web on mobile devices, etc.

5. Web 3.0 enhances customers' satisfaction with the help of 'artificial intelligence', web 3.0 helps the organization to improve the level of their customers' satisfaction in terms of customer relationship management (CRM). Through this, customers can have access to entire information about the product that is being offered by the company on its web page. This improves the company's image in the market and as a result, more customers can be attracted.

6. Web 3.0 helps to organize collaboration in social web nowadays, most people have registered themselves with the various social networking sites. Many weblogs have emerged as a part of these sites. by web 3.0, the information available can be linked through RDF. this process helps in creating a list of

conversations across blogs and mailing lists. with web 3.0, the users can experience a totally novel form of Internet because it can be accessed on different devices. it also offers a rich application tier with more logic.

WEB 1.0	*WEB 2.0*	*WEB 3.0*
The mostly read only web	The widely read-write web	The portable personal web
Focused on companies	Focused on communities	Focused on the individuals
Home pages	Blogs	Life stream
Owning content	Sharing content	Consolidating dynamic content
HTML, Portals	XML, RSS	The semantic web
Web forms	Web applications	Widgets, drag and drop mashups
Directories (taxonomy)	Tagging (folksonomy)	User behavior (meonomy)
Age views	Cost per click	User engagement
Netscape	Google	iGoogle, Net Vibes

3. LIBRARY 3.0

Libraries are moving along with the latest technologies. Readers' demands, staffing levels, service models, access to resources, and services to the public are also changing accordingly. Web 3.0 brings us great technologies such as semantic web, cloud computing, mobile devices, new social media applications and new search technologies. Library 3.0 refers to libraries using Web 3.0. It is a model for a modernized form of library services that reflects a transition within the library world in the way services are delivered to users. It refers to libraries using technologies such as the semantic web, cloud computing, mobile devices and re-envisioning our use of established technologies such as federated search to facilitate user-generated content and collaboration to promote and make library collections accessible.

3.1. Features of library 3.0

(a) Web OPAC

One of the key aspects of Library 3.0 is Web OPAC. A Web OPAC is a library catalogue on the Web or Intranet. Users can search the required information by connecting to Uniform Resource Locator (URL) of Web OPAC anytime during the day and from anywhere in the world. It is programmed to facilitate the library's members to access the OPAC through their own search for the ease of borrowing instead of searching through the card catalogue. In addition, members would also be able to request for the information about borrowing, reservation etc related to their own library profile, as well as to make automatic reservations. In Library 3.0, Web OPACs of various libraries which are forming a part of visible or invisible web would be brought together. Metadata of contents (contents in any format) would be seamlessly accessible and searchable from single user interface.

(b) Ontologies

Ontologies are used for annotating information to the web content and expressing its semantics in a machine-readable manner. These are the techniques to give richer semantic relationships between terms and thoughts of knowledge. These give more standardization in managing web contents instead of merely indexing the terms. Ontology aims at how the information is organized rather than organizing the information. These will be able to give more flexibility in providing semantic description to the content in learning object repositories and at the same time these facilitate automated functions and task delegation to intelligent agents. Ontology deals with questions concerning what entities exist or can be said to exist and how such entities can be grouped, related within a hierarchy and subdivided according to similarities and differences.

(c) Virtual Reference Service

Library professionals are obliged to serve the user community irrespective of their presence in the library, because technology is developing very fast in all domains. It is defined that, digital reference or virtual reference primarily refers to a network of expertise, intermediation and resources placed at the disposal of someone seeking answers in an online environment. In virtual reference service, apart from helping the users in personal or telephonic way, libraries are now developing the contents which can easily be transferable and readable in cellphones and other mobile devices to help users at any point of time.

(d) Semantic Web

The Semantic web provides a common framework that allows data to be shared and reused across applications, enterprise and community boundaries. Its objective is to convert all the unstructured documents on the Web into a web data. It is based on the Resource Description Framework (RDF). It will provide us with the option to share, unite, search and organize the web information in easy manner. Sharing and organizing information available in every corner of the web which is the main aim of this generation and expected to be achieved with the help of semantic web technologies.

The objectives of both the libraries and the Semantic Web are similar. Both of these have been developed for accessing information available in abundance and discovering the knowledge through cooperation and collaboration for the advancement of society. The use of Semantic Web technologies in developing Library Portals facilitates users' search, access and retrieval of learning resources. The portal should aim to provide access to a coalition of learning repositories with learning resources available in different formats. The implication of Library Portals with Semantic Web services will fulfill the vision of Libraries. The large collections of learning resources are semantically annotated adopting various technologies that facilitate user's access to the content in one or more learning repositories.

(e) Cloud Computing

Cloud Computing means using the Internet and central remote servers to maintain data and applications instead of maintaining data on individual mainframe computers or PCs. In short, cloud computing refers to the technologies that provide software, data access, storage devices that do not require physical location of the system. It is one of the most important Library 3.0 applications that is gaining popularity day by day.

Cloud computing technology offers great opportunities for libraries to build networks among the library and information science professionals as well as other interested people including information seekers by using social networking tools like 'Twitter', 'Facebook' which play a key role in building community power.OCLC is one of the best instances for making use of cloud computing for sharing libraries' data. Its world cat is the most popular online union catalogue for searching library data.

(f) Federated Search

Modern day searching is synonymous with Federated Searching which is one of the aspects of Library 3.0. It can help users to take greater advantage of online resources offered by libraries. Many online databases need different logins, look vastly different and search and display results in different ways. It would be easier for users to have all the search results displayed in one place and in one way , much as a Google Search does.

(g) M-catalogue (Mobile Library Catalogues)

The use of smart devices and mobile phones has increased dramatically over the past few years. All libraries should cater to users who access their library through their phones or other mobile devices. It can be made possible by either developing mobile apps or responsive feature of websites are to given. There is great potential for expansion of this technology in modern day libraries. More people are using mobile phones and devices as tools for tasks for which they previously may have used a laptop or desktop computer.

(h) Quick Response Code (QR Code)

QR code stands for Quick Response code. It is a two-dimensional bar code and can easily read by QR code reader software. It was first introduced in the year 1994 by the Denson Wave- Toyota Motors subsidiary. QR code can be read through device which has the QR code reader facilities like the mobile phones. Library uses it as a medium to communicate the users to their documents/ information that they want. The 21st century libraries are fully automated and they know the users' demands.

The main aim of using QR code is to give brief message to the users. There are several ways to use the QR code in Library environment.

- To give directions to the user
- To provide brief information to user
- To inform of required documents
- To promote the library services
- To create link to all the resources available in the library
- To create link to virtual tour of library sections
- To use in library exhibitions like Videos, Audios, and websites
- QR code is used to provide text messages for reference service and contact information of library staff as well as library patrons

	Web 1.0	Web 2.0	Web 3.0
Communication	Broadcast	Interactive	Engaged / Invested
Information	Static / Read-only	Dynamic	Portable & Personal
Focus	Organization	Community	Individual
Personal	Home Pages	Blogs / Wikis	Lifestreams
Content	Ownership	Sharing	Curation
Interaction	Web Forms	Web Applications	Smart Applications
Search	Directories	Keywords / Tags	Context / Relevance
Metrics	Page Views	Cost Per Click	User Engagement
Advertising	Banners	Interactive	Behavioral
Research	Britannica Online	Wikipedia	The Semantic Web
Technologies	HTML / FTP	Flash / Java / XML	RDF / RDFS / OWL

Fig. Comparison between web 1.0, 2.0 and 3.0

4. CONCLUSION

The utilisation of web technology to the library has enabled to become the LIS professional as information specialist. Web 3.0 technologies and ontology have enabled Library 3.0 and have brought about fundamental changes in the way the information is collected and disseminated. The role of the information professional are becoming more and more sensitive, the library professional will have to additionally learn about the related subjects along with the existing knowledge base. In this technology based and consumer based environment, there are enormous resources before the user community for catering their needs. So LIS professionals will have to move along with the technological innovations.

REFERENCES

1. O'Reilly, T. (2005). What Is Web 2.0: Design Patterns and Business Models for the Next

   Generation of Software [Online]. O'Reilly Media, Inc.http://radar.oreilly.com/archives/2006/12/web_20_compact.html.

2. Al Enezi, Ali K (2012). Library 3.0: the art of Virtual Library

services, Kuwait : University of Kuwait.

3. Anidhya Bhattacharya (2016). Library 3.0 and its implications in modern library services. *IJNGLT,* 2(1).

4. Lokhande,Rajesh Sahadeo (2016). Web 3.0 and Library 3.0. *International J. Advances in Social Sciences* ,4(1).

5. Waqar Ahmed, (2015) Third generation of the Web: libraries, librarians and Web 3.0, Library *Hi Tech News,* 2 (4),pp.6-8, https://doi.org/10.1108/LHTN -11-2014-0100.

6. Rudman, Riaan & Bruwer, Rikus (2014). Defining Web 3.0: opportunities and challenges. *The Electronic Library,* 34 (1), pp. 132-154.\

7. Devika Prabhu (2016). Application of web 2.0 and web 3.0: an overview. *International Journal of Research in Library Science,2,Issue (1), 54-62.*

8. Khanzode,Ku. Chhaya A. & Sarode, Ravindra D (2016). Evolution of the world wide web: from Web 1.0 to 6.0. *International Journal of Digital Library Services, 6 (2).*

2
Library App in Library 3.0: A Revolutionary Tool for Innovative Services in Library Environment

*Ravi Kumar Merugu**

1. INTRODUCTION

At preset everyone is using advanced mobile phones for a wide range of information and correspondence for their day to day life necessities. Current situation is man without mobile similar to a man without cerebrum. The access of mobile technology has been expanding in a wide

* Senior Library & Information Assistant, Sardar Vallabhbhai Patel National Police Academy, Hyderabad, Telangana.

range of individuals from child to old, uneducated to educated and poor to rich. Like in the library and information field too swung to adopting the most recent patterns and advances in giving quality services without technological hindrances. In this rising Information, communication and web environment, the library clients, data searchers and information seekers are imperatively relying upon digital resources or electronic resources for up-to-the-moment and well-run data.

In this information explosion era, the library services must be re-imagined according to client's needs and prerequisites. In general scenario, in all the financial transactions the latest technology playing a remarkable role like online payments, transfers, shopping, bookings, orders and other emergency services. In a similar way, libraries also should implement and get to use the human less services on finger tips. Then only the clienteles, library benefactors, information neediest would be satisfied.

The transformation of library services from traditional to computerization including digitization, virtualization, usage of social media, blogs and personal web sites are up to now. But, still a deficit in providing services through mobile technologies in almost all library information centres in India. It's time to bring out from library techies to enhance the library services without touching the computers. Then only the library primary objective will be fulfilled. That new technology in library field is called library App which will be incorporated voice call, video call.

Already all types of libraries have been playing major role for providing and distributing the required information to their users or clientele according to modernization and latest developments for research or innovative creations. In this aspect, libraries are transforming from traditional to computerization, digitization, virtualization and social media. But, still a gap is there between users and libraries in utilizing the valuable information which is disseminating from libraries. Hence, the new technology will to arise for closing the gap for maximum usage of library resources in single click through mobiles. Beyond the computerization, automation, digitization, virtualization and social media a tool should be needed i.e. "Library App" the most and energetic tool in present android environment for library service through mobile phones. It is a futuristic tool for smart library services.

2. HISTORY

In 1999 first time in the world, the Japan's company called NTT DoCoMo was introduced the mobile based library services for their library users. Toyama University library was made availability of OPAC access through mobile in September, 2000. It brought great recognition to their university. Later many colleges and university libraries were adopted mobile services and made provision to access the mobiles in the library with limitations against the library rules.

Actually few of mind hunting queries are arising. Those are

- Why we need a library app?
- Application of Library App?
- Features of Library App?
- Expectations for Users need?

3. WHY WE NEED A LIBRARY APP IN THIS EMERGING ERA?

Rapid changes in the library environment, we should provide innovative services through highly usage tool i.e. library app like circulation, reminders, renewals and reservation facilities, recommendations for new arrivals, e-material, bibliographies, circulation history, book availability information, articles details, catalogues, call numbers information, dial up facility, access of online resources, referral links, complaints, suggestions and feedback information.

As we said above para, the energetic and dynamic services in library environment a new tool must be needed. The users are unable to get leisure time to visit the library for adopting the require information. But, **A Library App** can replace all the drawbacks of existing systems including ICT / LMS / digital libraries / institutional repositories / Social Media and etc...would be disappeared, because this futuristic tool will be worked on mobile platforms. Users can access all the available resources with a click on mobile App without visiting the library or computer.

4. APPLICATION OF LIBRARY APP

Fig. Library App

Online Public Access Catalogue (OPAC)

It provides of all the bibliographical details of library material including books, course material, manuals etc... along with status of availability and checked out.

Circulation Module

It will do the all the housekeeping Operations including books renewals, reservations, circulation history, requisition and etc...

Through Periodical Modules

The users would be able to access online journals, article softcopies and archives along with latest issues.

By CAS/SDI module

The Library Clientele can know the latest material of the library including books / journals / documents and other allied material by time to time. And the users can get their require material through SDI services in stipulated time.

From the OPAC

The library customers can be known the bibliographical details of the library including status of the item.

News of the Library

This module gives the all the news of the library including latest arrivals, comments and events.

Alert Services

It will provide alert services of library i.e. reminders of received material, new arrivals availability, demand books and material information etc.

Suggestions/Comments

Through this module, users can offer suggestions on library services and material. And can give comments and may recommend books/periodicals also.

SMS/E-Mail service

This library can be provided SMS/E-Mail services for immediate effect on services for authentication.

5. FEATURES OF LIBRARY APP

Enormous features with library app are as follows.

- The vital advantages of library app is that access

the library without foot fall in library.

- The user can access library services through mobile app while in travelling, playing, working and eating also.
- It would be very flexible and comfortable to access the e-resources of a particular library.
- It's free of cost to download and access.
- Don't necessitate extraordinary skills to works with Mobile App; a lay man also can handle easily.
- It will be user friendly.
- It's very flexible tool compare to computer/desktop/laptop etc.
- Quick and accurate services will be got.
- It overcome's the geographical barriers.
- Economic burdens might be gone for procuring computers/desktops/laptops etc...
- Need not installation of network topology and other hardware inputs.
- Access all through 24x7

6. CONCLUSION

In this emerging, digital and IT era, the library scenario is necessitate to re-modify their structure, facilities and services to achieve the user's objectives and goals. The services of the library should be re-designed and re-shuffled according to latest trends and customs in this information explosion society from physical to computerization, computerization to digitization, digitization to social media and social media to apps. The apps in the library environment would be great revolution in library services to reach the client's needs and perks. All the modules of library provide the information with single touch on library apps. Now, the development of apps in the library field is initial stage. The techies would have huge opportunities to enlarge their skills and abilities to provide library services through library apps. The library app helps to get all the services including OPAC, CAS, reference services, renewals, reservations, latest arrivals etc.

REFERENCES

1. Washburn, Bruce. (2011). Library Mobile Applications: What Counts as Success?. Information Outlook *Vol* 15 Issue 1 (January/February). *http://www.oclc.org/research/publications/library/2011/washburn-io.pdf.*
2. Jim Hahn, (2012). "Mobile augmented reality applications for library services", New Library World, Vol. 113 Issue: 9/10, pp.429-38. https://doi.org/10.1108/03074801211273902
3. Aiguo, Li. (2013) "Mobile Library Services in Key Chinese Academic Libraries, Journal of Academic Librarianship.Vol. 39 pp.223-226, doi:10.1016/j.acalib.2013.01.009.
4. Nazi, Ayoob, Ghasempour, Sakineh and Asgari, Leyla (2014) "A Feasibility Study of Mobile Services Implementation in National Library and Archives of Iran: user's trends. *Library Philosophy and Practice (e-journal).* 1108. *http://digitalcommons.unl.edu/libphilprac/1108*
5. *http://libraryconnect.elsevier.com/articles/technology—content/2009— 11/go— mobile.*
6. *https://princh.com/8-technologies-to-implement-at-the-library-of-the-future/#.W-QQ1dIzZdh*

3

Library 3.0: Web Based Implications for Virtual Library Services in Digital Era

Durgaprasad A*

1. INTRODUCTION

Libraries are changing and customer demands are changing too. Staffing levels, service models, access to information resources, and services to the public are changing accordingly. Administrators are seeking more efficient ways of delivering services to achieve greater returns on financial investments.

* Assistant Professor, Library Science, Nagarjuna Govt. College, (Autonomous) Nalgonda, Telengana.

2. LIBRARY 3.0 REFERS TO LIBRARIES

The end result of Library 3.0 is collections that can be made readily available to library users regardless of their physical location. Library 3.0 is a virtual complement to physical public library spaces, and ideally will work seamlessly within established public library services and collections. With Library improvement, Libraries are trying to adopt Web 3.0 into their services through methods such as Resource Description and Access (RDA) tags, metadata and other semantic web developments. The semantic web has changed the face of the Internet, and will continue to change and develop the way libraries conduct their online services such as OPACs and federated searching. Librarians working in Library 3.0 environment are called Librarians 3.0 Library 3.0 is more than a building; it is a new philosophy of service and engagement for our community. It will be a place to interact; a place to innovate; a place to inspire. The author review papers discussed Web 3.0, Web 3.0 technologies, Library 3.0 and Librarian 3.0.

While the term is widely defined and interpreted, "Web 2.0" was reportedly first conceptualized and made popular by Tim O'Reilly and Dale Dougherty of O'Reilly Media in 2004 to describe the trends and business models that survived the technology sector market crash of the 1990s (O'Reilly, 2005). The firms, services and technologies that survived, they argued, all had certain characteristics in common; they were cooperative in nature, interactive, dynamic, and therefore the line between the creation and consumption of content in these environments was blurred (users created the content in these sites the maximum amount as they consumed it). The term is currently wide used and understood, but Web 2.0, primarily, isn't an internet of matter publication, however an internet of multi-sensory communication. It's a matrix of dialogues, not a group of monologues. It's a user-centered internet in ways that it's not been to date.

This characterization of the current state of the Web is at times contended, and though the clear delineation between the first and second Webs is here admitted to be rather arbitrary, it still must be recognized that the Web is really involving into a more interactive, multi-media driven technological space, and this understanding of the term is used in this paper. As O'Reilly (2005) observes in what is often cited as the seminal work on Web 2.0, personal web-pages are evolving into blogs, encyclopedias into Wikipedia, text-based tutorials into streaming media applications, taxonomies into "folksonomies," and question-answer/email customer support infrastructures into instant messaging (IM) services.

The implications of this revolution in the Web are enormous. Librarians are only beginning to acknowledge and write about it, primarily in the "biblioblogosphere" (weblogs written by librarians). Journals and other more traditional literatures have yet to fully address the concept, but the application of Web 2.0 thinking and technologies to library services and collections has been widely framed as "Library 2.0". Most writers on Library 2.0 would agree that a lot of what libraries adopted within the initial net revolution square measure static. For example, online public access catalogs (OPACs) require users to search for information, and though many are beginning to incorporate Web 2.0 techniques by gathering data regarding a user (checked-out things, most well-liked searches, search alerts), they are doing not respond with recommendations, as will Amazon.com, a additional dynamic, Web 2.0 service. Similarly, the1st generation of on-line library instruction was provided via text-based tutorials that are static and don't reply to users' wants nor enable users to interact with each other. These, however, have begun evolving into additional interactive, media-rich tutorials, mistreatment animation programming and additional subtle info quizzes. Libraries are already going into Web 2.0, however the move has just about begun.

Library 2.0: Libraries are emerging, Funding limits and customer demands are transforming staffing levels, service models, access to unutilized resources, and services to the public. Administrators, elite community, politicians and taxpayers are seeking more efficient ways of delivering services to achieve greater returns on financial investments.

Enter Library 2.0. This new model for library service is being elaborated online, at conferences, in administrative offices, and at the reference desk. If you and your library staff are not among those already talking 2.0, getting particular attention; Library 2.0 could revitalize the way we serve and interact with our customers. The heart of Library 2.0 is user-centered change. It is a model for library service that encourages constant and meaning change, inviting user participation in the creation of both the physical and the virtual services it is required, supported by consistently solving services. It also attempts to reach new users and better than current ones through improved customer-driven services. Every part by itself could be a step toward higher serving our users; but, it's through the combined implementation of all of those that we will implement Library 2.0. This increase in out there technologies provides libraries the power to supply improved, customer-driven service opportunities. have been playing a significant role in our ability to keep up with the changing needs of library.

Library 2.0 trends in collections, users and services: The goal of Library 2.0 is to bring the library nearer to the user

Library 2.0 - using Web 2.0 Tools to deliver library services:

- Blogs and Wikis
- RSS Feeds, MySpace/Facebook, Social Bookmarks, and Tagging

Difference between Library 1.0 and Library 2.0

Library 1.0	*Library 2.0*
Read only catalog	Catalog with user tags, comments, reviews (like WorldCat.org)
Print newsletter	Team built Library blog with RSS feed
Library instruction	Intuitive services
Walk in patron	Go to users (IM, podcastson Ipod, cell phone)
ILS is core operation	User services are core

3. IMPACT OF LIBRARY 2.0 ON LIBRARIES AND THE NEED TO LEARN ABOUT EMERGING TECHNOLOGIES

3.0. Web 3.0 is third generation of the web

Web 3.0 brings us great technologies such as semantic web, cloud computing, mobile devices, new social media applications and new search technologies.

Web 3.0 Technologies In today's Internet dominated world, every business organization has recognized the need for having an effective Web 3.0 site. In the present always-on world, a company's website plays a very critical role in competing with others and in attaining success.

The following are some of the technologies employed in Web 3.0:

- Artificial Intelligence.
- Automated reasoning.
- Cognitive architecture.
- Composite applications.
- Distributed computing.
- Knowledge representation.
- Ontology (computer service).
- Recombinant text.
- Scalable vector graphics.

- Semantic Web.
- Semantic wiki
- Software agent.

Some of the examples of Web 3.0 sites are **iGoogle**, **Net Vibes, Dig, Flicker, Delicious**.

A web 2.0 application is below

Blog (Web Log) : Blog could be a sort of website or part of an internet site. Blogs are a unit typically maintained by a private with regular entries of comment, descriptions of events, or different material like graphics or video. Entries are a unit ordinarily displayed in reverse-chronological order. Blog may also be used as a verb, aiming to maintain or add content to a blog.

4. ICONS OF WEB 2.0

a. Blogs User comments
b. Wikis
c. RSS feeds
d. User tagging
e. Social bookmarking
f. Social network Sites
g. Instant messaging
h. User comments, ratings, summaries
i. Podcasts, vodcasts citation services
j. Community photo sharing
k. Community book services (publishing) and Streaming audio and video

RSS : is another Web 2.0 application that helps users to bring the updates and feeds from different websites. It's a awfully easy tool to bring the newest stories, updates from news teams, magazines, journals and blogs. In an exceedingly recent study of Australian University Libraries, RSS was found the foremost wide applied technology (Linh, 2008).

It creates a feed from a website that readers will then add into associate to create one purpose of access for several sources (Davison-Turley, 2005).

Instant Messaging (IM) : Instant messaging (IM) may be a variety of communication over the web,, that provides fast transmission of text-based messages from sender to receiver. instant electronic communication primarily offers period direct written language-based on-line chat. The users text is sent over a network, like the wed. It's going to address point-to-point communications in addition multicast communications from one sender to several receivers. Additional advanced instant electronic communication permits increased modes of communication, like live voice or video calling, video chat etc...

Examples:

- Face book
- Twitter
- instant messaging
- E-mail
- chat rooms

Currie : states that libraries will offer on-line reference services by using employees staff at public desks throughout nights and weekends once the library is closed for different services.

Tagging : It would flip the useless "cookery" to the helpful "cookbooks" instantly, and lateral looking out would be greatly expedited.

Of course, tags and standardized subjects aren't reciprocally exclusive. The catalog of Library 2.0 would modify users to follow each standardized and user-tagged subjects; whichever makes most sense to them. In turn, they will add tags to resources. The user responds to the system, the system to the user. This labeled catalog is associate degree open catalog, a customize, user-centered catalog. It's library science at its best.

Wikis : wikis are a unit another example of cooperative artistic work. Multiple users from everywhere the planet will build a knowledge base by using this application. These tags are a unit terribly helpful for retrieving relevant pictures.

Mashups : Mashups are a unit may be the one abstract underpinning to any or all the technologies mentioned during this article. They're on the face of it hybrid applications, wherever two or a lot of technologies or services are a unit conflated into a very new, novel service.

Library 2.0 may be a mashup. It's a hybrid of blogs, wikis, streaming media, content aggregators, e-messaging, and social networks. Library 2.0 remembers a user once they log in. It permits the user to edit OPAC knowledge and data, saves the user's tags, IM conversations with librarians, wiki entries with different users (and catalogs all of those for others to use), and also the user is in a position to form all or a part of their profile public; users will see what different users have similar things checked-out, borrow and lend tags, and a large user-driven catalog is made and mashed with the standard catalog.

Experts views on Web 2.0

- Web 1.0 - place to go & get and Web 2.0 - place to be & do
- Introduction of the read/write web
- Interactive two-way web
- Everyday folks with Internet access can create and edit stuff
- Built on principle of breaking down barriers librarians placed on services

5. FEATURES OF WEB 2.0 TECHNOLOGIES IN LIBRARIES:

Proactive services : Librarians are already using tools such as blogs, wikis, RSS feeds, podcasts (in Apple iTunes), videos (in YouTube), photo sharing on Flickr, instant messaging via Meebo and Twitter.

Improved communications (internal and external): Social networking tools not only improve a library's communication withits librarians but they also improve internal communication andknowledge sharing.

Immediate implementation : Putt content on the net is not any longer the privilege for consultants with information of hypertext markup language and web programming languages, anyone will add on-line content. All you would like is access to a laptop.

Survival : Librarians should get on board the Web 2.0 wave. If they hesitate, alternative rival information services can do the task for them.

The Web 2.0 has revolutionaries the manner content is made and therefore the manner user's access, use and contributes data. Libraries are progressively adopting Web 2.0 technologies to style services that permit them to succeed in users within the virtual area that they may not reach before, this enables librarians to focus on a section of users within the population world health organization can never visit the library to use their services, notwithstanding however laborious they fight an outsized a part of this population belongs to the generation that grew up with web and that they are usually referred to as the digital natives. Rainie (2006) describes six realities of the digital natives as follows:

- Media and gadgets are common throughout daily life
- They get pleasure from media and keep on communications anyplace they need with the new gadgets out there to them

- Internet is at the middle of this transformation
- Multitasking is that the means of life , An standard national contains a larger chance to be a publisher, moviemaker, artist, song creator and storyteller

Everything can amendment even additional within the coming back years; we will expect additional computing power, communication power and storage power. Library collections currently embody a mixture of ancient materials (printed books, serials, audio-visual) and rising formats (e-books, e-serials, e-newspapers, e-dissertations, e-resources, digital objects, playa ways, streaming audio & video).

Library catalogs are group action access to any or all materials through next -generation On-line Public Access Catalogs.

Library 3.0 : Library 3.0 is more than a building. Libraries will provide information for their user wherever they are using the technology of Web 3.0. (Mi & Nesta, 2011) says "Library 3.0 must lead rather than follow and it must innovate, rather than copy". Library 3.0 must find ways to index and connect to all. Libraries need to change the way they interact with users. According to (Mason, 2011) In Library 3.0 the library comes to the patron, it is proactive and interactive.

In Library 3.0 is not only to provide the service to the people but it serves the user with various services. They should know how to get the requested information and make it available to the user without being concerned about the location. They should also help the users to make use of the given information.

Virtual reference service In virtual reference service, apart from helping the users in person or through telephonic ways, librarians are now developing the contents that can easily be transferable and readable in cellphones and other mobile devices to help the users at any point of time.

According to (Urban, 2010) Tito Sierra and Markus Wust, both from North Carolina State University Libraries were able to create virtual campus tour using geotagging (tagging specific locations on a map) and geolocation (pin-pointing your exact location) technologies. The writer said "Librarians must utilize new and upcoming technologies in order to reach twenty-first century learners" which author is highly recommend that.

6. CONCLUSION

Libraries are changing fast and constantly. Customer demands are changing, service models, access to resources, and services to the public. Library users are seeking more efficient ways of getting information. Library 3.0 is user-centered and a virtual complement to physical public library spaces. Libraries of the future will act like high-tech services companies, mini Google focused on a particular demographic and physical footprint. Libraries using Library 3.0 model will have the opportunity to be with user anywhere. You can call it Library in pocket. I think Library 3.0 is great development for libraries. Mobile Libraries and Virtual libraries are the next generation of Libraries.

REFERENCES

1. Abram, S. (2005). Web 2.0 - huh?! Library 2.0, librarian 2.0. Information Outlook, 9 (12), 44-46.
2. Breeding, M. (2006). Web 2.0? Let's get to web 1.0 first. Computers in Libraries, 26 (5), 30-33.
3. Casey, M. (2006b). Library Crunch: bringing you a library 2.0 perspective. Accessed May 18, 2006, from http://www.librarycrunch.com/
4. Crawford, Walt. (2006). "Library 2.0 and 'Library 2.0'" Cites and Insights, 6, 2. Accessed June 10, 2006, from http://cites.boisestate.edu/civ6i2.pdf
5. Del.icio.us. Accessed May 18, 2006, from http://del.icio.us/
6. Face book. Accessed May 18, 2006, from http://www.facebook.com/

7. Flickr. Accessed May 18, 2006, from http://www.flickr.com/

8. Habib, M. (2006). Conceptual model for academic library 2.0. Michael Habib's weblog on library and information science. Accessed June 10, 2006, from http://mchabib.blogspot.com/2006/06/conceptual-model-for-academic-library.html

9. Mashups (web application hybrids). (2006). Wikipedia article. Accessed June 10, 2006, from http://en.wikipedia.org/wiki/Mashup_(web_application_hybrid)

10. Miller, P. (2005b). Web 2.0: building the new library. Ariadne, 45 (October, 2005). Retrieved June 21, 2006, from http://www.ariadne.ac.uk/issue45/miller/

11. Peek, R. (2005). Web publishing 2.0. Information Today, 22 (10), 17-18.

12. RSS (file format). Wikipedia article. Accessed June 10, 2006, from http://en.wikipedia.org/wiki/RSS_(protocol)

13. Tebbutt, D. (2006). Is all the talk of web 2.0 just a lot of codswallop? Information World Review, (221), 9-9.

14. Varnum, K. (2006). RSS4Lib: Innovative ways libraries use RSS. Accessed June 10, 2006 from http://blogs.fletcher.tufts.edu/rss4lib/

PART-II

Open Source Library Software

4

DRUPAL (Open Source Software) : A Step by Step Installation for Implementing the Digital Library

Ravi Kumar Merugu

INTRODUCTION

In this digital epoch, the explosion of information and communication is overloaded and out of hold time to time. To all the aspects, issues and problems the human being are well depended on information. From the ancient to present the inventions, creations, developments,

* Senior Library & Information Assistant, Sardar Vallabhbhai Patel National Police Academy, Hyderabad, Telangana.

productivity of research come out from existing information only. In this yield of scientifical, technological and communal developments, the role of library, information, knowledge hub is unexplainable and uncountable. Earlier, the print format was dominated in all the areas of Developments but present digital format of information is playing a tremendous role in education and research field.

At present, the human beings are unable to consult the information centres directly to meet their required information due to time constraints. To wipe out this gap the digital libraries or virtual libraries or institutional repositories are born and brought. All most all the information of research productivity and educational needs are getting digitized and serving through online. In this remarkable modulation of service, the open source softwares are major tool to all types of information centres or libraries whether it is government or private. In present market many open sources softwares are available to digitize the library resources which are not commercialized, institutional contents, free material.

OPEN SOURCE SOFTWARE

After initiation of open source software system, the revolutionary changes have been cropped up in all areas of technical, research and education. The software developers make available of entire code of the software under the GNU General Public licence for free run and usage. It is not only for free utilization, also for modifying as per needs and necessities. A software developers provides code for free to modify, change, alter according to necessities of a particular entity is called 'Open Source Software'.

CMS (Content Management System)

Common origination of contents by utilizing a software application is called 'Content Management

System'. It is sorted out or shows the contents over websites or internet without having any learning of programming languages or web applications. All types of contents like texts, images, audio, and video contents can be customized in a simple way in CMS. The key feature of CMS is that simple to develop a library website with all the HTML effects through it modules, templates, layouts in shorter period.

DRUPAL (Open Source Content Management Software):

Drupal is Content Management free and open source software originally developed by 'Dries Buytaert' and initial version released on May 18th 2000. Now look after by Drupal community. It is a free application to create a web based application to enable the contents for wise utilization. It is user friendly application to handle, create, maintain and publish all types of contents under free interface called GNU General Public Licence.

Requirements for Installation of Drupal:

- Pentium PC (e.g. Pentium III 500MHz)
- Sufficient RAM for serving the network (e.g. 512 MB)
- Large and fast hard disk (e.g. 20 GB)
- Operating system: Windows 2000 Server or Windows XP Professional or Linux
- Optional: networked DVD-ROM drives
- MS-SQL Server 6.5

Attribute of this Article

- Simple steps to installation of Drupal.
- No assistance to installation.
- Trouble-free understanding.
- Without confusion
- No require of software skills
- No need to get training to installation

- Further, take assist from drupal community
- No require DVDs/CDs to installation

Step by Step process for 'Drupal' Installation

In the process of 'Drupal Installation' concentrate on Do's & Don'ts

Do's

- Disable the antivirus software
- Sufficient memory in 'D' Drive
- Firewall permissions while in installation (if IP is on intranet system).
- Require high speed internet connection
- Avoid confusion for operating system (Windows/ Linux) while in installation.
- Power backup facility
- Keen observation while installation
- Follow the steps
- Authenticate Username and Password
- Remember the Username and Password to open drupal
- Proper inputs according to installation steps.
- Disable 'Cloud server' option for installation while in process.

Don'ts

- Don't do other works while in installation.
- Don't use mobile while in installation.
- Don't refresh the system while in installation
- Don't leave chair while installation
- Don't remove or change key board/mouse while in installation.
- Don't power off
- Don't disable the internet connection

A Step by Step Process of Drupal-CMS Installation

A systematic approach herewith elaborated for simple and easy way to install 'Drupal-CMS' open source software for implementing the digital library. Follow steps carefully.

Step-1

Just type in Google as **'bitnami'** and press enter as showed in figure 1.

Fig. 1. 'bitnami' at google browser

Step-2

Click on 'Drupal' option which is third one among 6 options or

Go through Drupal Website and select 'Drupal'

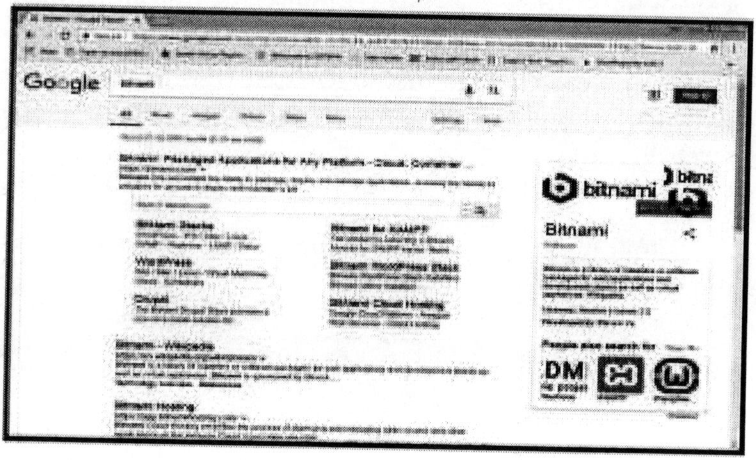

Fig. 2. Options in Google

Then you will get following menu.

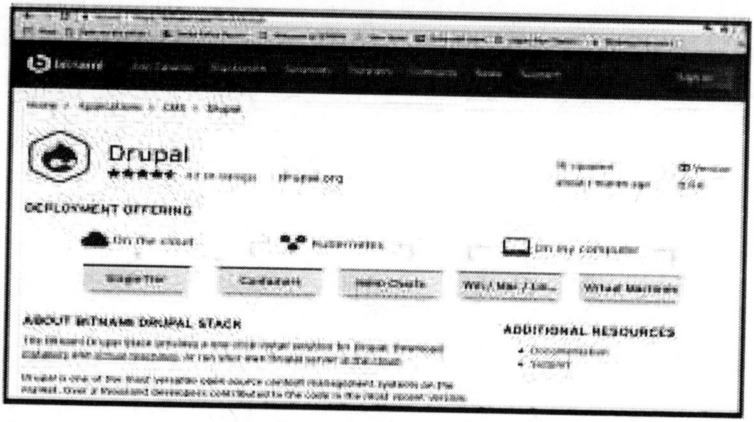

Fig. 2.1. Deployment Offering

Step-3

Click on any option among the 5 to start downloading Drupal software.

Here the installation process described on windows operating system platform to understand all in easy way.

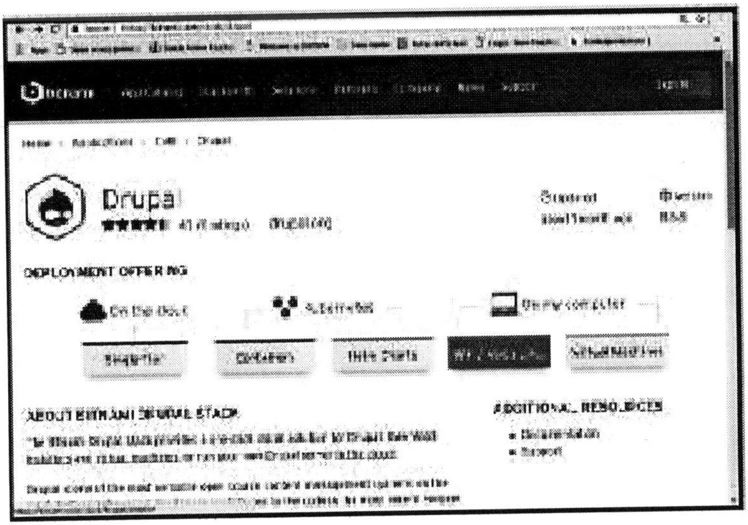

Fig. 3. Select Win/Mac/Lin....

Step-4

Then click on **Download for window/OS x......** option to get the process of downloading.

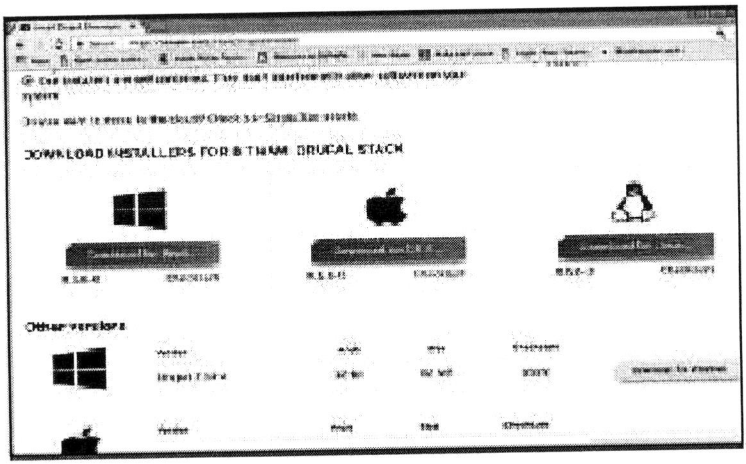

Fig. 4. Download for Windows/OS x.....

Step-5

When click on the '*Download for Window*', would get the below menu.

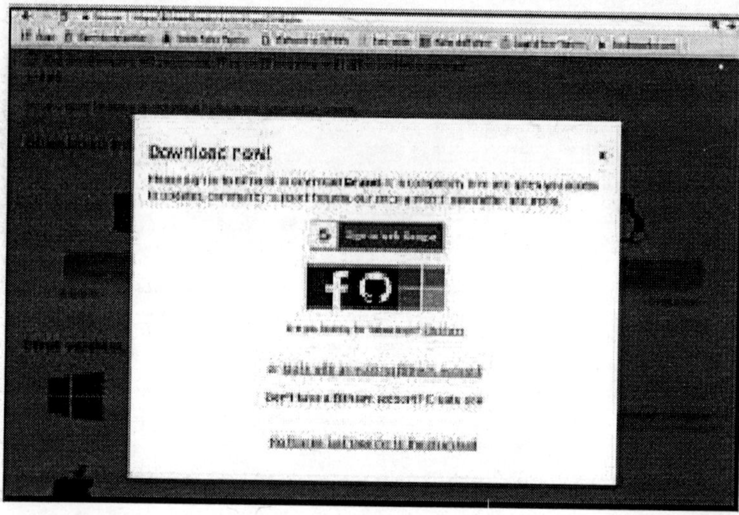

Fig. 5. Select No Thanks

Step-6

To download Drupal files you might have sign in with Google/Face book etc... OR click on '*No Thanks, just take me to the download*' option to get files.

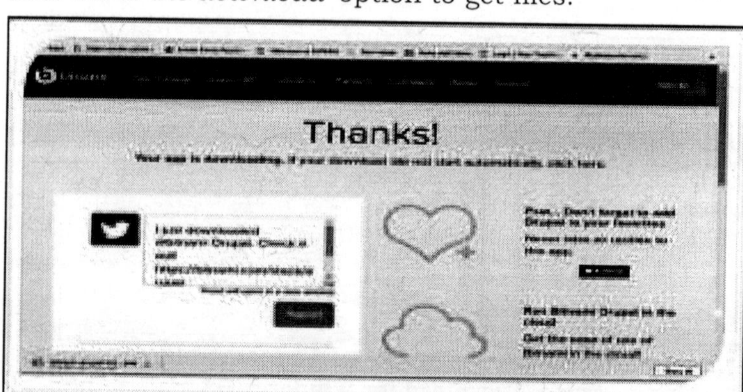

Fig. 6. Thanks

After downloading of the files you will get the above screen with THANKS.

Step-7

Next, go to download folder and open the bitnami-drupal folder to install.

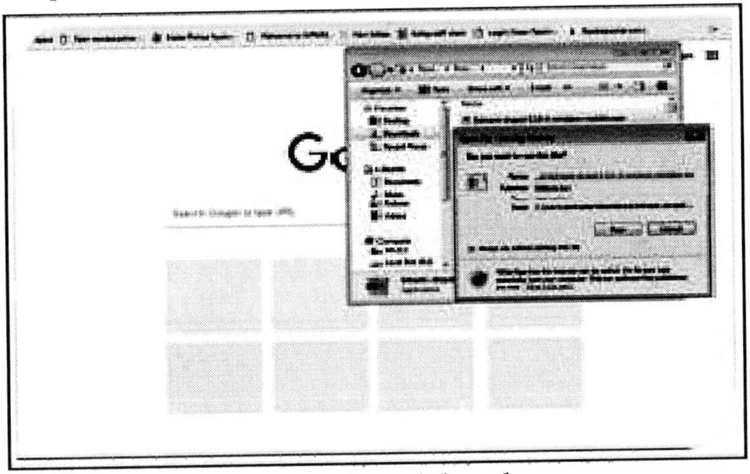

Fig. 7. Bitnami-drupal

Step-8

Then click on *Run* option to follow the installation steps.

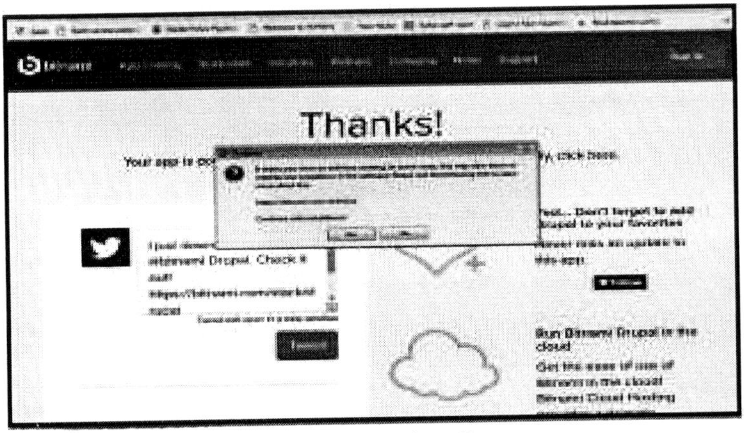

Fig. 8. Installation Steps

Step-9

After clicking on *Run* option, just click on *Yes* to start the installation.

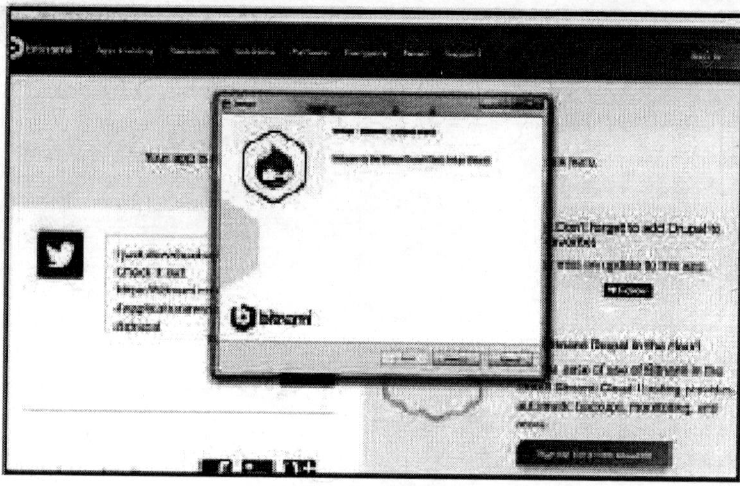

Fig. 9. Setup

Step-10

Select '*Drupal & PhpMyAdmin* options, then click on *Next* button

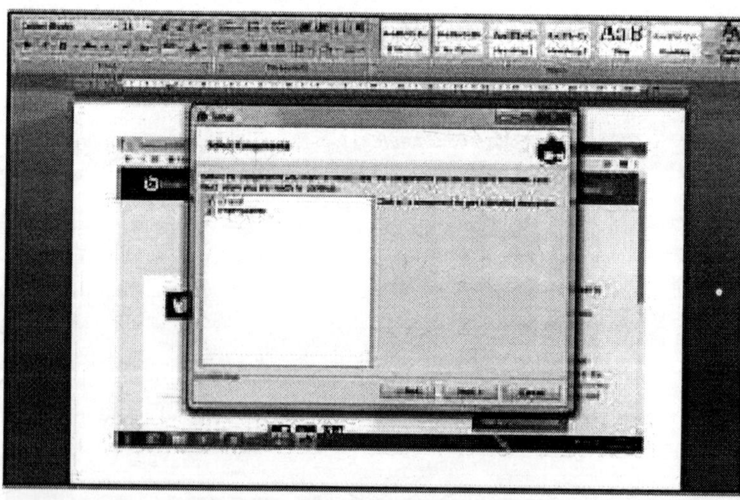

Fig. 10. Drpal & PhpMyAdmin

Step-11

In this menu, choose drive for installation. Better to choose 'D'drive. Then click on *Next* option.

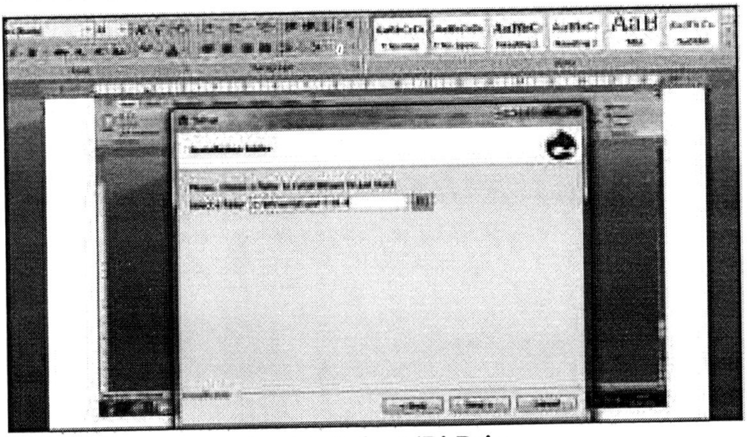

Fig. 11. Select 'D' Drive

Step-12

Next, this below setup menu will ask user creation details i.e. Real Name and working email for further communication. Must be assured proper Login ID and Password and then only on *Next* button.

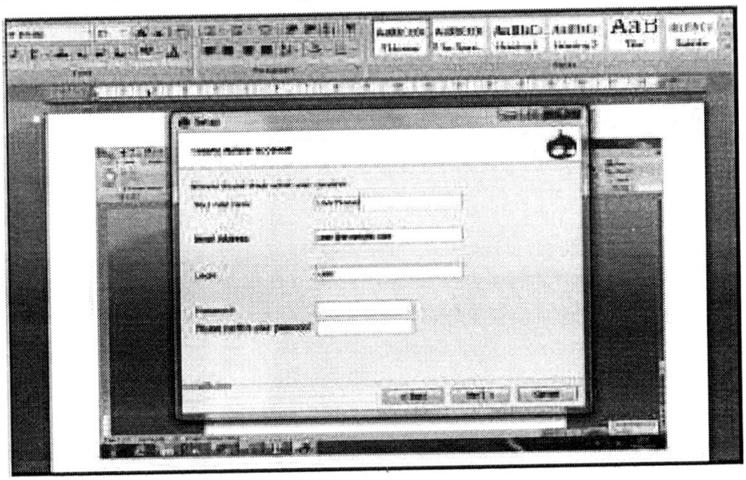

Fig. 12. Login ID and Password

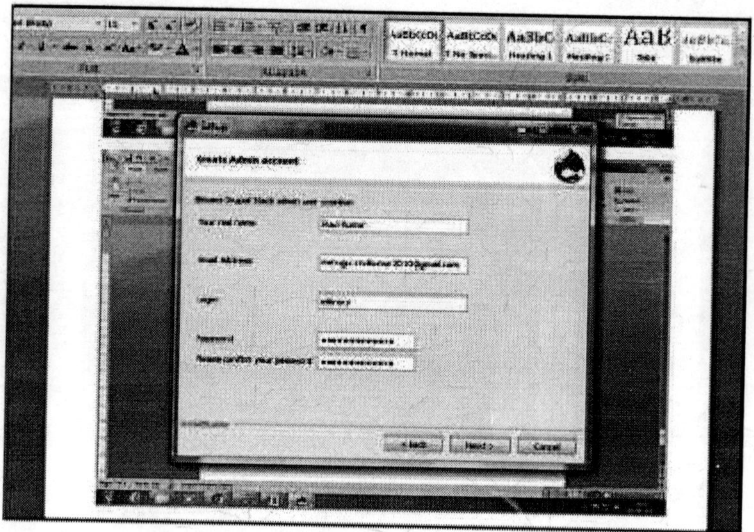

Fig. 12.1. Proper login ID & Password

Step-13

After proper inputs for login and password, '*Drupal site Name*' must to add. Here given eLibrary@ravikumar for example.

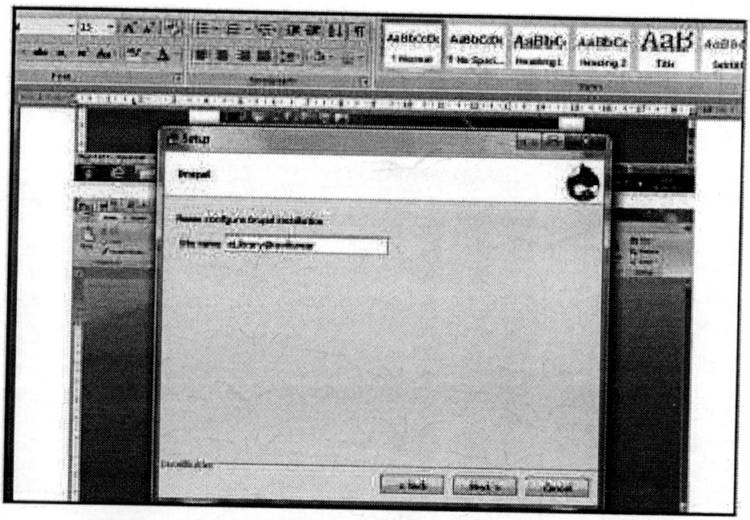

Fig. 13. Drupal Site Name

Step-14

Next it asks 'Launch drupal in the cloud with bitnami'; Suggested to disable the click option to installation in local server.

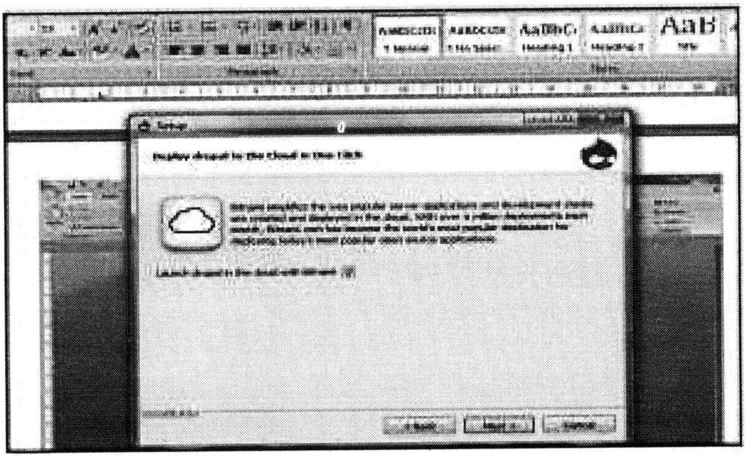

Fig. 14. Cloud Installation Option

Step-15

The following screen appears to click on *Next* button for installation the drupal

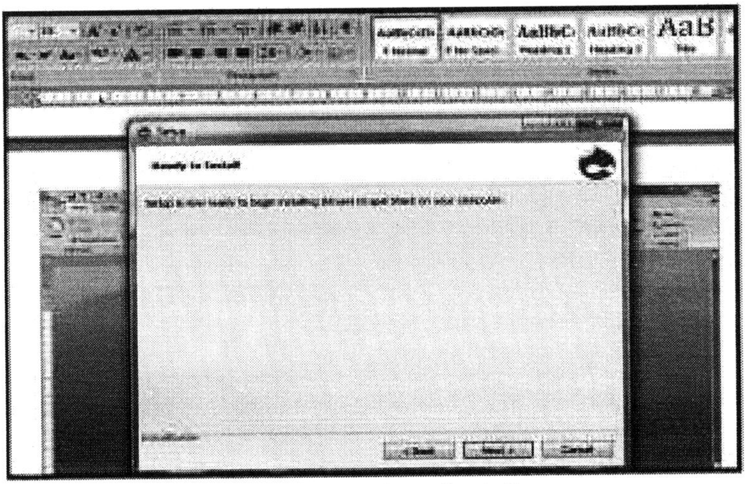

Fig. 15. Ready to Install

Fig. 15.1. Installing Process

Step-16

Drupal installation will finish by clicking on to 'finish' option.

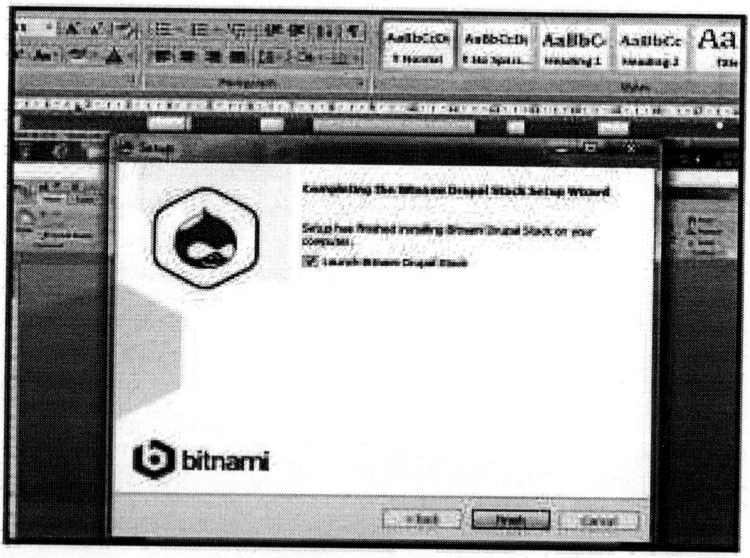

Fig. 16. Finish

Step-17

After completion of installation process, will get the following menu, then close it.

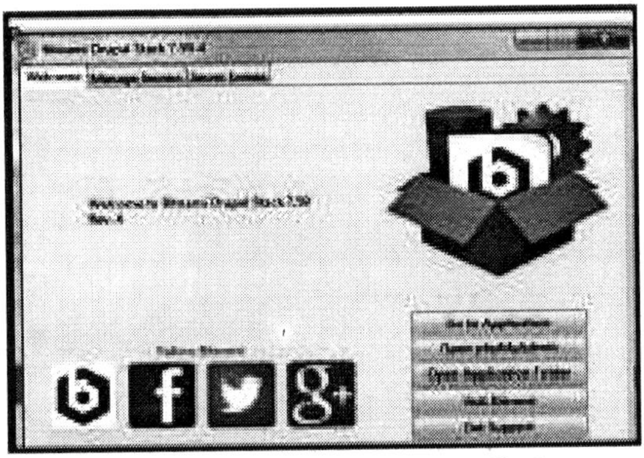

Fig. 17. Successfully Installed

Step-18

Now open browser, then enter *localhost/ drupal* press enter. Will get drupal home page successfully with site name as showing under below box.

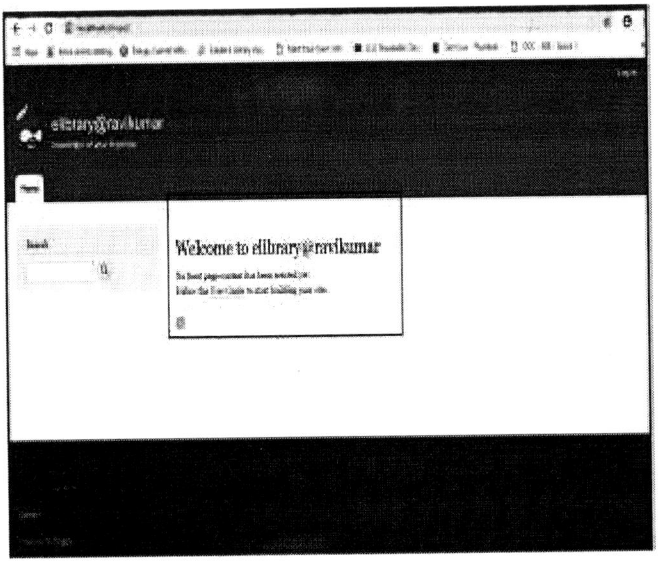

Fig. 18. Drupal Home Page

CONCLUSION

Development of digital library is a vital and important aspect in library & information field to hold up the electronic resources of the library in a systematic and standard layout. In this process, elaborated the installation method by using Drupal (open source CMS) with uncomplicated and understandable manner with step by step process along with screen shots. Moreover, descriptions also consolidated with all the screen shots to pursue the procedure for avoiding redundant confusion and mystification while in installation. Dupal CMS is a user friendly and dynamic with adding new versions time to time for graceful appearance and broad convention. All kind of library experts can introduce this product without help of any software specialists, framework directors and other technicians.

REFERENCES

1. https://bitnami.com/stack/drupal
2. Patnaik, Rachna & Mishra, Mukesh Kumar (2018). Implementation of Drupal: An Effective Content Management System for Space Applications Centre Library, ISRO, Ahmedabad. Kaul, H K, Mani, G Naga Ratna, Kaul, Sangeeta. (Eds.), Knowledge, library and information networking (NACLIN) 2018 (pp. 20-36). New Delhi: DELNET.
3. Ravi Kumar Merugu (2016), implementation of library automation: a creative approach. Research India Publications, New Delhi.

5

Execution of Library Automation through Open Source Software (NewGen Lib): A Personal Experience on NewGenLib Software

Gatla Krishna Reddy
Muduganti Deepthi Reddy

* Librarian, S.K.N.R Govt. Arts & Science College, Jagtial, Telangana

** Librarian, Alphores Womens Degree & P.G. College, Karimnagar, Telangana.

1. INTRODUCTION

Library and information center is considered as heart of any institution and soul of any teaching and learning institution. With the advent of information communication technology (ICT) there is a paradigm shift from traditional libraries to automated and digital libraries. Academic library is a treasure house of knowledge and it plays very important role in the explore of information. Technology has become as the culture among the stakeholder in all walks of life due to the reach, the cheaper cost, multiplication, virtual reality and easy to use. Automation is an immense process for any system including higher education and institutions. The term Automation was first concerned by D.S Harder in 1936.Automation is a process of using the machineries for easily working and saving the human power and time.

Library Automation refers to the use of computers to serve the needs of the patrons of the library. Traditional library work consisting of acquisitions, technical processing, serials control, circulation and reference services all entail time consuming manual work. The operations of a library get a quantum jump with the introductions of computers. The computers help to provide fast and reliable access to the resources available in the library as well as elsewhere. The application of computers in the library operations avoids repetitive jobs and saves lot of manpower, time, speeds up operations, increases use of library resources. Computers are not only used as a tool for processing the data, but also for data storage and accessing.

Automating a college library is the process which restructures its functions and reinvents its services. By keeping a database as the basis, automation converge new technologies of information storage and retrieval with traditional housekeeping operations. An automated college library can serve the teaching and learning community more effectively. A reduction in the time needed for routine operations can be utilized to give customized services to the users.

2. LIBRARY AUTOMATION NEED AND NECESSITATE

Even though this question seems to be very fundamental it is essential to emphasize this aspect, as the library automation is yet to take off in majority of the Government Degree College libraries in Telangana. Secondly, while justifying need for library automation more than cost-effectiveness the benefits derived by the patrons become the major consideration. To appreciate the advantages it becomes necessary to highlight the different levels of library automation.

Following are considered as important factors for Library Automation

- Information explosion
- Increase in the collection of libraries. (Library is a growing organism)
- Advances in the computer and communication technology
- Wastage of user / staff time in locating the information (Save the time of the patron)
- Provide wide access to resources within the libraries and elsewhere (With the help of OPAC- Open public access catalogue)
- Better Access, Quality in service and Co-Operative efforts (Resource Sharing)

3. WHAT IS OPEN SOURCE AND OPEN SOURCE SOFTWARE

The term "open source" refers to something people can modify and share because its design is publicly accessible. The term "Open source software" is software with source code that anyone can inspect, modify, and enhance according to their requirements.

4. STATUS OF LIBRARY AUTOMATION IN TELANGANA GOVERNMENT DEGREE COLLEGES

So many factors may be considered to do automation of the college libraries in Telangana. The process of Government Degree College's libraries automation started from 2005 in both the telugu states but only few colleges completed the total automation process in Telangana. In the year 2005 in the combined state of Andra Pradesh 126 colleges selected as pilot project and all the selected colleges librarians trained by UGC-INFLIBNET at Hyderabad. The INFLIBNET centre provided SOUL (Software for Universities Libraries) software to all these colleges and collegiate of higher education sanctioned all the ICT infrastructure which required to run the SOUL software. . One time settlement done to INFLIBNET SOUL software from the CCE, till date there is no up gradation of the software and there was no annual maintenance paid to the INFLIBNET.

One DTP operator assigned to the library for data entry process but most of the colleges not continuing the DTP operator in the libraries. Almost all the 126 colleges provided by SOUL Software done the data entry of books in the SOUL software up to 2009 purchased books only.

Majority of govt. degree colleges in telangana is having internet connections and sufficient ICT infrastructure to do library automation like scanner, barcode readers(minimum one), laser printer, higher configuration systems (recently TS govt. sanctioned six lakhs rupees to all GDC's) towards purchase of computers.

With the above table we came to know that only three colleges are using open source software, and with SOUL software only three colleges completely automated, remaining colleges partially completed the library automation process.

5. STATEMENT OF THE PROBLEM

With the paid and proprietary software's the colleges are facing so many problems the major problem is financial burden to the colleges, paid software's are charging the annual maintenance very huge amount and up gradation charge will extra, the service is depend upon the financial commitment whereas using with the open source software the software and the code is freely accessible from the net and the annual maintenance, if required is very less as comparatively with proprietary software, and by using with the blogs and forums we can solve our problems whenever we required. With the help of our students and SRR Family we want to do library automation with the open source software that is NEWGENLIB. The project started in October 2016. This project is entitled as Complete Library Automation using with Open Source Software (NEWGENLIB).

6. OBJECTIVES OF THE STUDY

- To know about how to do Library Automation using with open source software
- To know about the data conversion (i.e. from MYSQL to POSTGRESQL)
- To Explore the Library Automation Process.

7. LIMITATIONS OF THE STUDY

The study is limited to Government Degree College only. The study covers like Budgetary resources, open source software NEWGENLIB, ICT Infrastructure & Library Automation Services conversion of library data from sql server to postgresql, etc.

8. BUDGETARY RESOURCES FOR GOVERNMENT DEGREE COLLEGE LIBRARIES IN TELANGANA STATE

The Government degree college libraries primary source of income for collection development is UGC grants.

The UGC provides assistance to the college libraries only when college is enlisted under the Section 2(f) and 12 (b) of UGC Act. Recently Telangana government collegiate of higher education released special budget for all colleges to develop digital library. Under this scheme CCETS sanctioned six lakhs rupees amount to purchase computers, and depend upon the students strength CCETS sanctioned in the academic year 2016-2017 i.e. Rs.50,000 to Rs.5,00000 (five lakhs) amount towards purchase of text books, reference books and furniture.The other source is students special fee fund it is not sufficient to meet the recurring requirements of library.Govt degree colleges also receive Gifts from the alumni and the donations from the local leaders.

9. OPEN SOURCE SOFTWARE 'NEWGENLIB'

NEWGENLIB (NGL) open source library management software is an outcome of collaboration between Verus and Kesavan Institute of Information and Knowledgement management. NGL is developed and maintained by Verus Solutions and Kesavan Institute has provided the domain expertise.

10. NGL ADOPTION PROGRAM

Verus Solutions has started "NewGenLib Adaptation Program". You may also recommend this program for other libraries. This program is for libraries which are planning to automate their libraries in just 4 days. This is time-bound program. The duration of this program is 32 hours (4 - days). And it is very simple. There are schedules for this program. If you strictly follow the schedule you will fully automate your library in just 4 days. You will be visually observing your users' (and management) satisfaction and praise for library services. For further details to adopt NGL please see the website http://www.verussolutions.biz/web/

11. SOFTWARE AND HARDWARE REQUIREMENT TO INSTALL NGL SOFTWARE

a. Min requirements of the Server

Hardware: Pentium 4 or higher configuration, minimum 4GB RAM and minimum 80GB Hard disk

Software : Windows 2000prof, 2000 Adv Server, XP Home, XP Prof, Windows 7, Windows 8 and 2003 server or higher versions.

b. Min requirements of the Client

Hardware : Pentium 4 or equivalent, 1GB RAM and 40GB Hard disk

Software : Windows 2000prof, 2000 Adv Server, XP Home, XP Prof, and 2003 server, Red Hat Linux all versions. Before going to install NGL software you have to download Java latest version, Postgres SQL, and Install NGL. These files you can able to download from the following website link.

http://www.verussolutions.biz/web/content/download

12. ICT INFRASTRUCTURE AND LIBRARY AUTOMATION (SRR GOVT. ARTS & SCIENCE COLLEGE)

The process of SRR Government Arts & Science College library automation started from 2005. Funding for automation process provided by CCE for purchase of Computers, and the software provided by the INFLIBNET, i.e. SOUL software. One time settlement done to INFLINET SOUL software from the CCE, till date there is no up gradation of the software and there was no annual maintenance paid to the INFLIBNET. The software provided by INFLIBNET is limited edition software it is not useful for the 50,000 books and above. SOUL full version with latest edition is cost about Rs 80,000 and the annual maintenance for this software is Rs. 11,500.

One DTP operator assigned to the library for data entry process but this college is not continuing the DTP operator since 2012. SRR GDC done the entry of books in the SOUL software up to 2009 purchased books only.The SOUL database prepared in MS SQL. Only 21541 catalogue records (Books Details) entered in that database no issues done with the SOUL software.

Only two systems allocated to SOUL software. At present seventeen systems are available in the library including two server systems. One server is allocated for NEWGENLIB software and another one is for DSpace. All the systems are connected through LAN (Local area Network). Recently fourteen high configuration systems received to library from CCETS. Three barcode readers, one printer cum scanner, one laser printer and 10mpbs bandwidth speed internet is available in SRR GDC library.

After the careful examination with the above mentioned parameters SRR Govt. Arts & Science college Sri Sathavahana library has chosen NEWGENLIB (NGL) open source software to do its library automation. Data migration done from MS SQL to Postgres SQL by taking with the help of DATA MIGRATION tools available in the net. First I collected the mdf and ldf files form the SOUL server and retrieved 123 tables from the SOUL data back up. From that 123 tables only two important tables retrieved there are Biblidetails and Location table. In biblidetails table all the catalogue details is available in six coloums and one catalogue occupies minimum 24 to 26 rows depend upon the data filled by the cataloguer. Using with the transpose function(it is available in paste special option) we can make the each catalogue (24 rows) in to (24 coloums).

Below figure 12.1 gives the fields information available in the bibledetails table we need to take fvalue row.

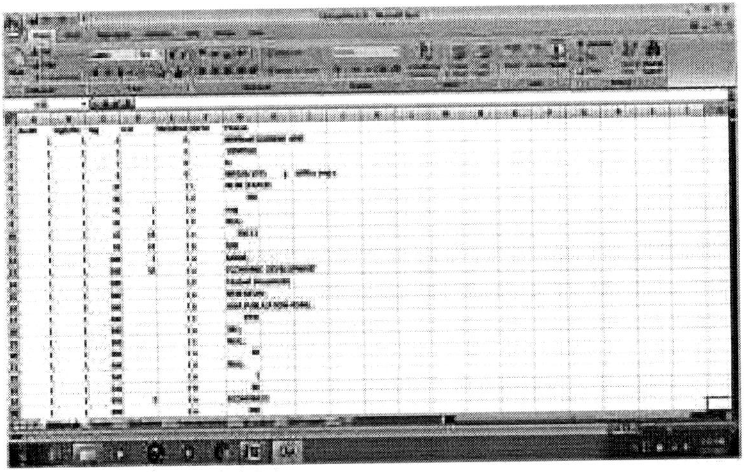

Fig. 12.1. Bibledetails table retrieved from SOUL backup

Below figure 12.2 gives clear information (column wise) about ACC.NO, Classification NO, Book NO, Cost, etc. but it doesn't gives the data about Author, Title, sub title, Joint Author etc. we can retrieve the total data from the above table 12.1

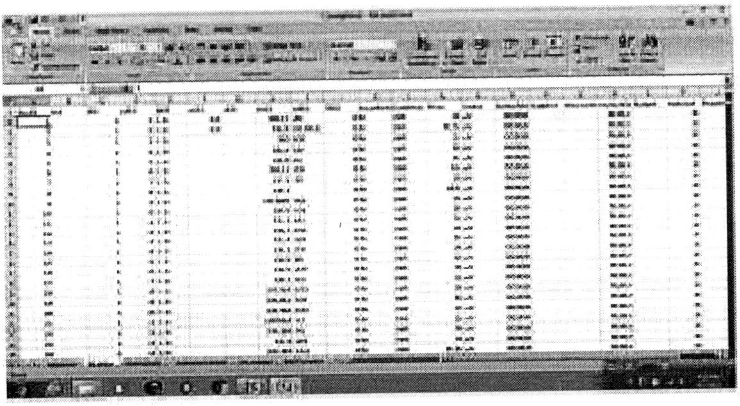

Fig. 12.2. Location table retrieved from SOUL backup

Below figure 12.3 gives information about how to create the single row catalogue in to multiple columns using Transpose function which is available in paste special. It Explains that how to extract the data from the table 12.1 bibletable, first take only the value row and using transpose function crate rows for each and every catalogue daily we can make 300 catalogue rows. After creating the total data table now it is the time to create conversion of the total catalogue records into csv file.

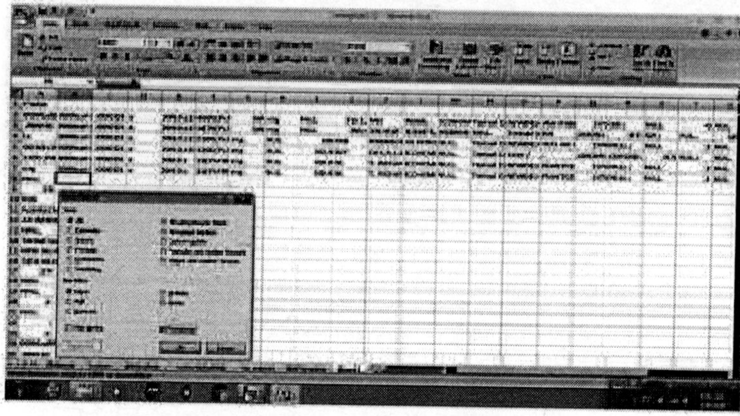

Fig. 12.3. Execution of value row using with Transpose function

It is possible to convert daily 300 records in to csv file(same as excel) so our srr college library SOUL records had been taken 21 days to convert all the catalogue records. The patron's details I had taken from the university web site directly. The whole patron's records (approximately 2500 records) stored in csv file. Three to four days time taken to retrieve the patron's data from the university website directly.

Below figure 12.4 Blank catalogue csv file in NEWGENLIB software, as per the heading we have to create the rows from the data available from the 12.3 and 12.2 tables. After creating the csv catalogue file we can upload n number of catalogue records directly from the NGL workbench app which is available with NGL3 software.

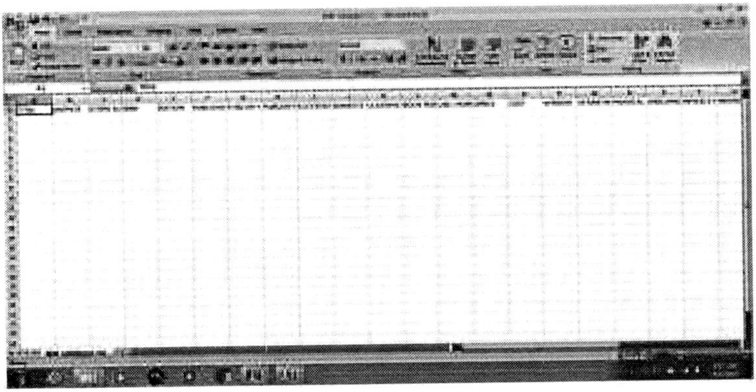

Fig. 12.4. Blank CSV file

Fig 12.5 import of n number of catalogue records through csv file from NGL workbench app, first go to NGL work bench app and go to utilities, import catalogue records, select the csv file path and select the file where we created in 12.4 figure the hundred records appears in preview section select import button depend upon the data it will create the catalogue records in database.

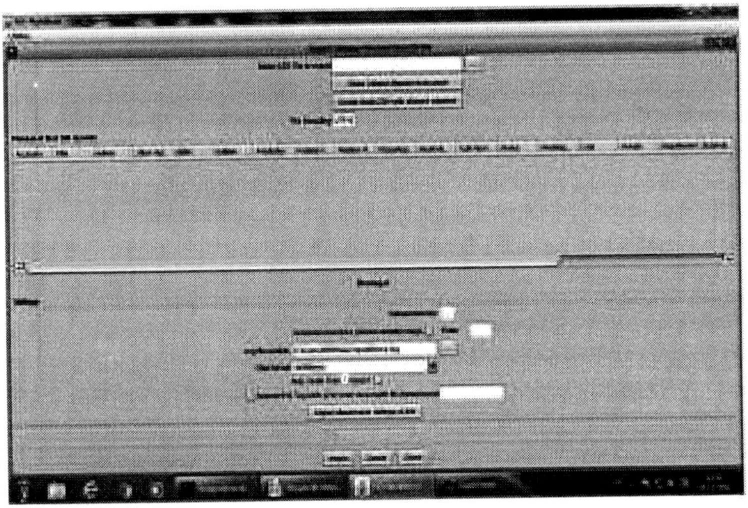

Fig. 12.5. Bulk import of catalogues using NGL workbench through CSV file

After creating the catalogue record it will not reflect in the OPAC as well as in the search status to reflect in the OPAC we have to run the index file which is available in the C drive automatically it pools the data and all the catalogues will be available in OPAC.

13. OPAC SERVICE BY SRR GDC LIBRARY

The OPAC module is a patron module,OPAC (open public access catalogue) gives the information about available books in the library. Patron can search with the title, barcode, author or subject wise etc. user can know about his circulation details and he can renewal, reservation the books directly from OPAC.

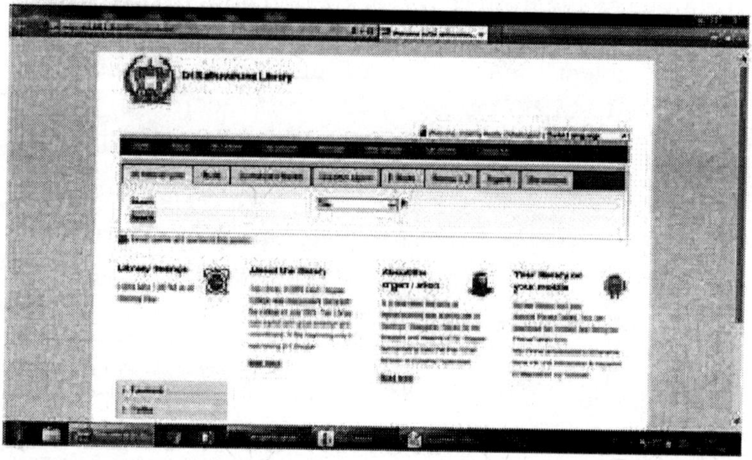

Fig. 13.1. Shows the OPAC screen of SRR GDC

14. INSTITUTIONAL DIGITAL REPOSITORY OF SRR GDC

Institutional Digital repository of SRR govt arts and science college build with open source software i.e. Dspace. Under this project we already uploaded the soft copies of 12 PhD thesis, 17 MPhil dissertations, 21 Minor Research Projects, more than 150 articles and our staff and students projects as well as previous question papers.

Within few weeks we are going to add E-BOOKS to our IDR, it is available for the benefit of our students and staff. Below fig. is the home page of SRR GDC Institutional repository home page.

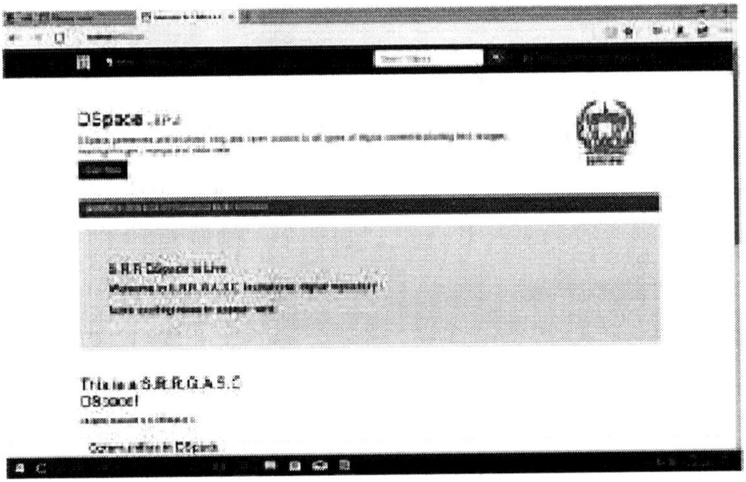

Fig. 14.1. Home page of Institutional Digital Repository of SRR GDC

Fig. 14.2. Communities in Institutional Digital Repository of SRR GDC

15. NGL MOBILE APP

By using this mobile app patron can search there library collection directly from their phones. And through **My Library** module user can see his/her check out books (Borrowed books), and user can reserve the books through this NGL Mobile app.

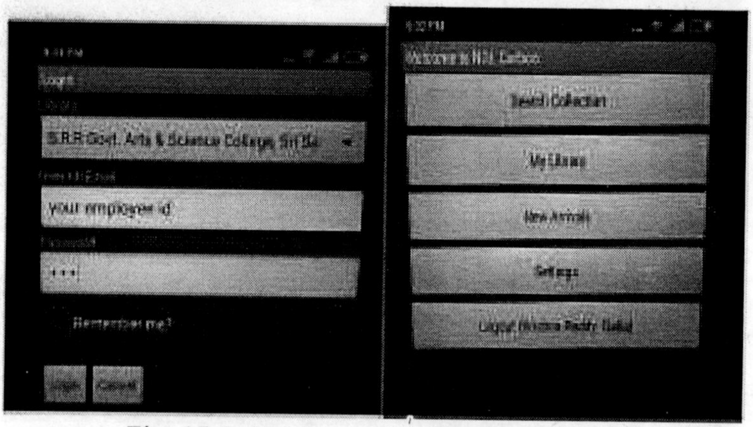

Fig. 15.1. Mobile app of SRR GDC library

16. CONCLUSION & SUGGESTIONS

After completion of this project Complete Library Automation using with Open Source Software (NEWGENLIB) My experience with S.R.R Govt. Degree College Sri Sathavahana Library. We observed the following few things.

The study concludes that academic libraries should adopt the latest technologies in there libraries to save the time of the reader in getting the information. All the GDC college librarians and the library staff need sufficient training programmes to update their knowledge.

1. Data Conversion may be difficult to the trained librarian, proper training may be required in migrating the data or it should be advised to engage the technical person to manage in the process of data migration.

There is a need to start certificate and bachelor courses in well established college libraries, and there should be compulsory internship to the student to work in the library so that they could get good practical knowledge as well as the libraries will get relief in getting manpower in their libraries.

2. Lack of resources and expertise, NGL is a open source software even though, with the available resources in Govt. Degree Colleges there is a chance to corrupt the software with viruses. It should be better to take annual maintenance from the service providers, they are charging very nominal amount for it.

   CCETS should take necessary steps in allocating the special funds to all GDC's and regular monitoring should be done to implement the latest technologies in Govt. degree college libraries.

REFERENCES

1. http://www.verussolutions.biz/web/
2. http://www.highereducationinindia.com
3. www.ugc.ac.in
4. www.inflibnet.ac.in
5. https://java.com/en/download/
6. https://www.postgresql.org/download/
7. Courant PN, Griffiths RJ (2006). Software and collaboration in higher education: A study of open source software. Organization for Open Source Software Study. Available at http:// www.ithaka.org/strategicservices/oss/OOSS_Report_FINAL.pdf.
8. Dhamdhere S (2011). "ABCD, Open Source Software for Modern Libraries", Chinese Librarianship: an International Electronic Journal 32 Available at: http://www.iclc.us/cliej/cl32dhamdhere.pdf.
9. Commissionerate of collegiate education government of Telangana website https://ccets.cgg.gov.in/
10. N-List National library and information services for

infrastructure for scholarly content website http://nlist.inflibnet.ac.in/

11. SRR Govt Arts & Science college library report submitted to NAAC SSR report in march 2017. http://gdcts.cgg.gov.in/karimnagar.edu
12. SRR Govt. Arts & Science college, certificate course in library & inf. Sc. Course broucher 2017. http://gdcts.cgg.gov.in/karimnagar.edu
13. Kulkarni, S.A. Best Practices in College Libraries. *National Seminar on Library and InformationServices in Changing Era,* 22-23 January 2009. p.273-281

6

Two in One: NewGenLib Software is a Paradigm for Library Automation and Digitization

Dodle Rajeshwar

1. INTRODUCTION

In olden days libraries are only for preservation purpose and later allowed the public utilization then allowed to barrow the books to read at home. Computer has its very impact upon libraries also due to its vast power of working different operations automatically without the intervention of the human. So it has changed the whole structure and working environment of the libraries. Library automation makes the things easier of

* Librarian, CMR Engineering College, Hyderabad, TS

library staff in their routine library housekeeping operations and also for users. Library automation needs proper planning which indicates the methods of support both internal and external, so that all components should work in coordination and can achieve the set objectives. Later library automation switched to RFID system to theft control of library books. RFID System is costlier but libraries can able theft control. Library software developers also develop the Library Mobile App for the benefits of its users.

The aim of the concept in this paper is to describe "One Software Two Benifits: NewGenLib Software is a Paradigm for Library Automation and Digitization." with facilities of library software and all modules of library functions with digital library facilities. There are different software available in the market for making library automation and digital library. Every library need to maintain two different servers, where as in NewGenLib library software there are two facilities in one software. NewGenLib supports library automation also digital attachments.

2. DEFINITION OF AUTOMATION

Library automation means the applications of various types of machines to perform the different routines and jobs involved in functions and services of the libraries. Library automation involves acquisition, cataloguing, classification, circulation, binding management and serials management. Nowadays all libraries are trying to do library automation to facilitate access to a small or huge amount of collection. Automated library has advantageous over the manual library.

Automated libraries reduce time in the repetitive processes of the libraries and reflect their holdings and users can able to do different types of search which is not possible in the traditional library system due to physical limitations. Computerization changes the whole structure and working environment of the library. The skills required to manage automated library are different from the required skills to manage a traditional library.

There are different types of software are providing for library automation. In some of them are commercial which libraries have to purchase and others are open source software. Open source software are easily available on the internet and can be freely downloadable and can be installation.

Most of the library software are developed based on RFID, Electromagnetic, Hybrid Technologies and Cloud Computing to taking new level of libraries for automation and security. A library professional to be need to training on a purchased software or open source software otherwise it is very difficult to maintain library automation. NewGenLib Library software is available both as open source and commercial and it supports all the above new technologies.

3. DEFINITION OF DIGITIZATION

Berkeley defines "Digital Library is a collection of distributed information sources, producers of the information make it available and consumers find it perhaps through the help of automated agents". Digital libraries are heterogeneous in nature. Digital Libraries digitize information, store, find, link, visualize, use, publish, manage and share information. Traditional libraries are owed new technologies to sustain in the digital era. In modern days the resources are available mostly in electronic forms and their functions are accomplished automatically. These libraries today are also called by other names such as digital library, virtual library, library without walls, paperless library tec. There is a widespread interest and development, lot of research activities are being published in digital form. Digital library provides access to very large collection of information, supports multimedia content and supports traditional library collection development, organization, access and preservation. Digital libraries are providing information in electronic form and it can be easily search and retrieve the information. Digital libraries disseminate information across a network and the users can retrieve information in the same way.

4. NEWGENLIB LIBRARY MANAGEMENT SOFTWARE

NewGenLib is a Library Automation Software outcome of collaboration between Verus and Keshavan Institute of Information and Knowledge Management in 2005. NGL is developed and maintained by Verus Solutions and Keshavan Institute has provided the domain expertise.Functional modules are completely web based and compatibility with international metadata and interoperability standards like MARC 21, MARC XML, Z39.50, SRU/W, OAI PMH uses open source components. NGL Library Automation software is scalable, manageable and efficient and it supports Windows and Linux operating systems and it supports other languages includes international languages. NGL can data entry, storage, retrieval in any language and also it supports RFID integration. Through the NGL software we can able to send SMS and e-mails of library transactions automatically.

4.1. System Configuration and Hardware Requirements

2 U Rack Servers

Xeon Dual Core 2.8 * 2 Processors,

8GB Ram

3TB external Harddisk

Raid 0,1,5

Dual RPS

Keyboard

Mouse

4.2. Acquisition

Library staff can use this acquisition module to send books and journals orders by online and can able to receive the orders in proper way. But before using this module library staff can be defined the budget of the each department. In practical most of the libraries face difficulties when giving order and receiving the order and at the end of financial year it should be adjusted the balanced amount. So, most of the librarian cannot use this module.

4.3. Serials Management

To maintain journals and to searching in OPAC we are creating catalogue records in serials management. Through serials management we can give order and we can create catalogue entry of a serials. In this NGL software we easily creating and maintaining serials. After creating catalogue entry of a serial we have to setup caption, pattern and create enumeratc, chronology then we can entry of the particular issue.

4.4. Web OPAC

There are various types of searches includes basic, advanced and expert search. NGL library software develops three different themes of OPAC in NGL 3.1.4 versions. In OPAC page library can keep their logo or banner on the header to create a new looks and attracts the users. It can also available on intranet or internet and supports smart phones. So, users can easily access library OPAC desktop and mobile phones. Recently Discovery tool added to the OPAC page, when we search for a title, subject the discovery tool gives results of related search term from subscribed e-journals or open access journals articles and in search results e-mail record or add record buffer (search result added in this feature, users can attach all the bibliographic records of searched results to their e-mail at one time) facility provided. List New Arrivals display through the New Arrivals tab and it gives option to view by number of days and if we click any title it shows complete bibliographic details of a document also facilitated. These new arrivals list can also be possible to send e-mail to users account. It also provides Top Stories of News Papers heading through RSS feeds.

4.5. NGL Library Mobile App

NGL Library App supports only on android phones for those who are using NGL Library Software. Carbon app can be downloading from the https://m.apkpure.com/carbon/org.newgenlib.carbon, IP and port to be need settings. If you want access OPAC within the campus, the IP must connected to the Wi-Fi or public IP should be given to connect the library server from anywhere, anytime. Through this app library users can be able to search and retrieve the library holdings of a particular library and also they can know the new arrivals added to their library and they can check their account status.

4.6. Other Features of NewGenLib Software

RSS Feeds : NGL OPAC also provides Top Stories of any one news paper heading through RSS feeds. It depends on news paper link provided by the library.

Union Catalogue : NGL software compiles union catalogue of different institutions in one group or participating libraries and displays search results in OPAC and show of the availability of library holdings with institution name and location. It can be useful for sharing information and using other library resources easily under inter library loan

Bar Code Printing : NGL Workbench facilitates to take barcodes with college name and logo print out for the documents on A4 size paper and we use it for library transactions.

CONCLUSION

The study concludes that when selecting the library software for automation and digital library software need not go for two different software for different purpose. It is better to select one software for easy upload documents and retrieve access easily and maintenance also can do easily. Academic libraries should adopt the latest technologies in there libraries to save the time of the reader in getting the information. All the Engineering college librarians and the library staff need sufficient training programmes to update their knowledge.

REFERENCES

1. Ravi Kumar.M (2016), Implementation of library automation: a creative approach, pp.152, Research India Publications, New Delhi.
2. http://www.verussolutions.biz/web/
3. http://www.libsys.co.in/
4. https://koha-community.org/
5. https://duraspace.org/dspace/
6. http://cmrec.ac.in/libraryabout.html

PART-III

Knowledge Management and Data Mining

7

Knowledge Based Approaches to Knowledge Management in Knowledge Society

Durgaprasad. A

1. INTRODUCTION

Knowledge has become driving force for social development and people's demand for more information and knowledge is increasing day by day. Knowledge based society library has become a treasure house of human knowledge. Knowledge management play a crucial role in the currently developing global knowledge society. The efficient utilization of professional knowledge is the vital factor of business in every country worldwide. Consultancy

* Assistant Professor, Library Science, Nagarjuna Govt. College,(Autonomous) Nalgonda, Telengana.

firms as well as special departments or institutions in enterprises represent the permanently growing of well-established knowledge industry or economy.

First of all new knowledge has to be developed in organizations, therefore a collective innovation-learning in organizations is presented. In this conditions of possibility concerning of innovation are discussed. Thus structural conditions are analysed which have to be fulfilled, if organizations are to succeed. Alavi and Leidner (2001) viewed Knowledge is increasingly recognized as a critical organizational resource, and in recent years many organizations have engaged in the development and implementation of systems to manage it through knowledge management systems.

Hansen et al. (1999) mentioned prescription for effective knowledge management is that an organization should adopt a standardized, homogeneous approach to knowledge management across the units of the organization. Yoo and Ginsberg (2003) examine how inter-unit differences in a global organization influence the knowledge sharing practices.

> "*Tomorrow's societies will be knowledge societies. Tomorrow's markets will be knowledge markets. Tomorrow's wars will be fought not by the conventional weapons, guns, missiles and so on, but they will be fought in the knowledge markets with the new thermonuclear weapons called information and knowledge*" (Mashelkar).

2. DATA, INFORMATION AND KNOWLEDGE

The role of knowing as part of action in creating new tacit (explicit) knowledge with the aid of explicit (tacit) knowledge, and one have identified but not justified, that information is a significant part of knowledge management. To support the focus on information as a critical resource for the creation of new knowledge, one will now try to illuminate the concepts of data, information, and knowledge and clarify their interrelation. This will shape the direction of the rest of the view.

3. DATA AND INFORMATION

Data is "a set of discrete, objective facts about events" describes part of what happened without relation to other things. As a result, data provide no justifications or interpretations. According to Peter Drucker "information is data endowed with relevance and purpose". In other words information can be acquired from data by giving them meaning in terms of relational connections. So data can be seen as the raw material for the creation of information. However, although information provides the meaning inherent in the relations between data, it cannot provide an explanation of "why" the data is what it is.

4. INFORMATION AND KNOWLEDGE.

Information is a means for communicating a message that is able of changing the receiver's perception of a situation and affect his judgements and Information can provide the receiver with a new way of interpreting objects and events by highlighting unexpected connections and implying unconsidered constraints What both Nonaka and Davenport imply is that information is a necessary material that aids in eliciting and constructing Knowledge. More specifically "information is commodity capable of yielding knowledge, and what information a signal carries is what we can learn from it. Knowledge is identified with information produced (or sustained) belief". The four human related activities that can result in the creation of knowledge based on the information received. These activities are:

Comparison : how does the information received under this context compare to previous situations.

Consequences : what are the implications (e.g. constraints or new insights) the received information has on the decision process of the current situation (context).

Connections : what are the relations of the received information to other bits of information

Conversation : what do other people think about this information It is evident by the above activities, that information's perceived meaning and thus the knowledge that can be created based on it, is dependent on context and that the receiver (his beliefs and commitment), his situation and his social interaction define this context. So the same piece of information can "give birth" to different knowledge, according to the context of the receiver. At the same time it is within the human receiver and his interaction with other humans that the above activities take place.

5. CORE ACTIVITIES OF KNOWLEDGE MANAGEMENT

Research and practice of knowledge management recognized following core activities of knowledge management:

- *Knowledge generation*
- *Knowledge sharing*
- *Knowledge utilization*
- *Knowledge storage*

Since the knowledge is a very general category it seems to be difficult to give its adequate definition. Especially in the context of its quantification and following possibility of knowledge measurement! But exactly this is the essential goal of knowledge evaluation – to find out the value of every single piece of knowledge. Particularly based on the determined value of professional knowledge enterprise management can identify the knowledge value of a single employee and make various decisions, e.g. regarding salary, business process organization, further qualification etc. Because of the market orientation of each product or service every enterprise is interested in objectivity of applied approaches for knowledge evaluation. This objectivity becomes indispensable under conditions of growing globalization.

At the same time, to define standards for a knowledge management concept that will work in practice.

The following are basic aspects to define the concept.

Compatibility : Knowledge management requires both a shared language and a good fit with concepts that already exist in the organization, such as Total Quality Management or Business Process Reengineering.

Problem Orientation : Knowledge management has to make a contribution to the solution of concrete problems; it must not be allowed to remain theoretical. The ultimate test of ideas is their usefulness in practice.

Comprehensibility : The company must choose terms and ideas of knowledge management that are relevant to its success and readily understood across the company.

Action Orientation : Analyses in the field of knowledge management should enable managers to evaluate the impact of their instruments on the organizational knowledge base and should lead to focused action.

Appropriate Instruments : Focused interventions need proven instruments. The final goal of a knowledge management concept is to provide a range of such instruments.

Before investing heavily in the development of new capabilities, can organisation should know what knowledge and expertise exist both inside and outside their own walls. Most big companies lose track of their internal and external data, information, and capabilities. This lack of transparency leads to inefficiency, uninformed decisions, and redundant activities. Restructuring, downsizing, and reengineering activities have increased this organizational opacity in many cases by destroying effective informal networks. Effective knowledge management creates sufficient internal and external transparency and supports employees in their knowledge-seeking activities.

Drew, (1999) few of the idea need to look in to the recommendations that made in many conference/ seminars is the following:

- Preparation is everything! Combine thoughtful analysis with careful consideration of practical issues.
- Avoid philosophizing and academic abstractions.
- Avoid developing integrated knowledge architecture at first attempt.
- Look for better ways of doing things the organization
- Build knowledge networks and communities of practice around important problem areas. Integrate knowledge management with the firm's strategy.
- Seek the full support of top management and the board.
- Align evaluation and incentive systems with knowledge sharing

5.1. Knowledge Acquisition

The explosive growth and simultaneous fragmentation of knowledge have made it all but impossible for companies to build up all the know-how they need for market success by themselves. Instead, they have to buy critical capabilities, often from many knowledge markets, using focused acquisition strategies.

5.2. Knowledge Development

Knowledge development consists of all the management activities intended to produce new internal or external Knowledge on both the individual and the collective level. The process of individual knowledge development relies on creativity and on systematic problem solving. Creativity maybe called the chaotic component of the knowledge development process and the capability of problem solving the systematic component.

5.3. Knowledge Distribution

In making knowledge available and usable across the whole organization, the critical questions are: Who should know what, to what level of detail, and how can the organization support these processes of knowledge distribution? Not everyone needs to know everything. Technical knowledge distribution infrastructures can support efficient knowledge exchange within organizations and connect formerly separated experts through an electronic network. Relevant technologies are groupware, modern forms of interactive management information systems, and all instruments of computer-supported cooperative work. Efficient knowledge distribution can generate not only time and quality advantages, but a direct rise in customer satisfaction. Distributed organizational knowledge stocks make knowledge available at various places in the company and support fast reactions.

5.4. Knowledge Use

Meaning the productive deployment of organizational knowledge in the production process in fact is the purpose of knowledge management. The successful identification and distribution of critical knowledge does not ensure its daily use. And without consistent use, there is a high probability that new knowledge systems will decay in quality, and the investment will be wasted. The potential user of knowledge has to see a real advantage in order to change his or her behaviour and "adopt" the knowledge

5.5. Knowledge Preservation

After knowledge has been acquired or developed, it must be carefully preserved. Many companies complain that in the process of reorganization they have lost part of their corporate memory. This collective amnesia is often the result of the unthinking destruction of informal networks. To avoid the loss of valuable expertise, companies must shape the processes of selecting valuable knowledge for preservation, ensuring its suitable storage, and regularly incorporating it into the knowledge base

5.6. Knowledge Measurement

The evaluation and measurement of organizational knowledge presents the biggest challenge in the field of knowledge management. In contrast to finance managers, knowledge managers have no tested tool box of accepted indicators and measurement processes. They are pioneers. And the subject they need to measure is particularly elusive. Knowledge and capabilities can rarely be tracked to a single influencing Variable. Furthermore, the cost of measuring knowledge is often seen as too high or socially unacceptable. Nevertheless, knowledge measurement holds considerable potential value, as has been demonstrated in a related field by human resources managers, who have had to prove the impact of training investments.

6. CONCLUSION

Knowledge is the most vital factor in the development and growth of individual persons and institutions also. The conventional role of library and information professionals was to collected, process, disseminate, store and utilize information to provide multidisciplinary services to the personal and professional needs of the library users. In the rapidly changing information and knowledge era, knowledge and information assets are available in the form of databases, knowledge bases, filing cabinets and in the minds of people knowledge and information are the basic assets in the personal growth. Librarians as knowledge managers. KM helps library and information professionals in improving the services being rendered to their users. Information professionals have to recast their roles as knowledge professional. The librarian's roles should not be limited to being the custodians of information but they have to acquire skills to keep themselves updated so as to cope intelligently and objectively with the effective and efficient KM in libraries. LIS Professionals in order to meet the challenges of the Knowledge economy are to build a KM system for Libraries which demand an urgent attention.The new knowledge Management should be very careful to gauge the commitment and culture.

REFERENCES

1. Alavi, M. and Leidner, D.E. "Knowledge management and knowledge management systems:Conceptual foundations and research issues," *MIS Quarterly* (25:1), 2001, pp. 107-136.
2. Hansen, et al (1999) "What's your strategy for managing knowledge?," *Harvard Business Review* (77:2), , pp. 108-116.
3. Yoo, Y.,and Ginsberg, M. (2003). "One Size Does not Fit All: Knowledge Management Systems and Knowledge Sharing Practices in Global Learning Organizations," Case Western Reserve University, USA .*Sprouts: Working Papers on Information Systems*, 3(12).
4. Drew, Stephen (1999) Building Knowledge Management into Strategy] Making Sense of a New Perspective , Drew, Stephen (1999)
5. Mashelkar R.A. http://www.entovation.com/kleadmap/RMashelkara.html

8

Data Mining in Library and Information Services

Dr. Akhtar Hussain*

1. INTRODUCTION

During the agricultural and industrial society libraries were one of the main sources for individual seeking information. After a period of uncertainty, during which it was perceived that the shift was taking place from 'industrial' to 'post-industrial' society or 'information' society, the nature of the society has become specious. According to Branscomb Information Society is "a society where the majority of people are engaged in creating, gathering, storage, processing or distribution of information". With the increasing demand for information, the focus of libraries has been to build large collection and repositories for knowledge in the form of print media. The innovation of IT have made the accessibility and storage of information so much easier and faster that the

* Assistant Librarian, NIEPID Regional Centre, Gautambudh Nagar, Noida.

demand for right user at the right time. The implementation of ICTs in libraries and information centers provide a variety of documentation and information services to support R&D, industrial productivity management, marketing and trade and all other programs of development emanating from autonomous, government and non-government and academic institutions. These information services can broadly be categorized into anticipatory and responsive services. Some of the important services which have been evolved as a result of developments in computer and communications technologies are: (i) Current Awareness Services, (ii) Online Search Services, (iii) Printed Indexes, (iv) Database Products and Services, (v) Document Delivery Services and CD-ROM databases.

2. DATA MINING

The information society era, the patrons are accessing information resources and library services through cloud computing or Internet. The Internet is a massive, searchable, dynamic widely available, distributed, multi-platform information system having a great potential of resources. The libraries today are challenged to provide their clients with the right source of information and services they require, and this has been made possible with the technique and process of data mining. Data mining is specific to produce information based on the patterns generated by the data captured in the systems. With the data mining systems, libraries can have the right resources, better services, the ability to strengthen their collections and information for the decision-making process.

Data mining (sometimes called "Knowledge Discovery in Databases" process, or KDD) is the process of analyzing data from different perspectives and summarizing it into useful information-information that can be used to increase revenue, cuts costs, or both. KDD have formed a branch of applied artificial intelligence (AI), since the 1960s. During the intervening decades, important innovations in computer systems have led to the introduction of new technologies for web-based education. Data mining allows a search, for valuable information, in large volumes of data. It allows users to analyze data from many different dimensions or angles, categorize it, and summarize the relationships identified. Technically, data mining is the process of finding correlations or patterns among dozens of fields in large relational databases.

Data mining is the exploration and analysis of very large volumes of data stored in a company's existing databases, or in repositories, such as data archives and data warehouses, to discover meaningful new correlations, patterns and trends. The development of new algorithms to cope with very large datasets has made it possible to exploit information that was stored, but to all objectives and purposes unusable. The process uses statistical techniques and pattern recognition technologies. It is essentially a mechanism for identifying data, on the basis of specified terms and associated terms and concepts, from a wide range of sources, so as to address complex problems.

2.1. Definitions

Data mining is defines as "the automatic extraction of useful, often previously unknown information from large databases or data sets".One of the popular definitions for "data mining is the process of exploration and analysis, by automatic or semi-automatic means, of large quantities of data to discover meaningful patterns and rules".Data mining can be defines as "An information extraction activity whose goal is to discover hidden facts contained in databases. Using a combination of machine learning, statistical analysis, modelling techniques and database technology, data mining finds patterns and subtle relationships in data and infers rules that allow the prediction of future results. Typical applications include market segmentation, customer profiling, fraud detection, evaluation of retail promotions, and credit risk analysis". This can be simplified as a process of getting information or knowledge from large amounts of data.

The field of data mining is still relatively new, and in a state of evolution. The First International Conference on Knowledge Discovery and Data Mining ("KDD") was held in 1995, and there are a variety of definitions of data mining. A concise definition that captures the essence of data mining is: "Extracting useful information from large datasets" (Hand et al., 2001).A slightly longer version is: "Data mining is the process of exploration and analysis, by automatic or semi-automatic means, of large quantities of data in order to discover meaningful patterns and rules".

Berry and Linoff later had cause to regret the 1997 reference to "automatic and semi-automatic means," feeling it short changed the role of data exploration and analysis. Another definition comes from the *Gartner Group of the information technology research firm* (Jan. 2004). "Data mining is the process of discovering meaningful new correlations, patterns and trends by sifting through large amounts of data stored in repositories, using pattern recognition technologies as well as statistical and mathematical techniques."

In other word we can say that the data mining process is to extract information from a data set and transform it into an understandable structure for further use. Aside from the raw analysis step, it involves database and data management aspects, data pre-processing, model and inference considerations, interestingness metrics, complexity considerations, post-processing of discovered structures, visualization, and online updating.

3. DATA MINING & KNOWLEDGE EXTRACTION

In information era, each and every day, people are

dealing with vast amount of data present in different formats. People are making decisions by analysing these data. Data mining is a process of extraction of useful information and patterns from huge data. It is also called as knowledge discovery process, knowledge mining from data, knowledge extraction or data /pattern analysis.

In information age, knowledge is becoming a fundamental organizational resource that provides reasonable advantage and giving rise to knowledge management (KM) initiative. Many organizations or libraries and information centers collect and stores huge amount of data. However, they are unable to discover valuable information hidden in the data by transforming these data into valuable and useful knowledge. Managing knowledge resources can be a challenge. Data mining is a process of sorting and picking out meaningful and useful information from a large pool of data.

Through data mining we can identify the trends or patterns of the data, thus we can propose a corresponding and optimum plan for the enterprise. As a part of data mining research, this paper focuses on surveying data mining techniques used in knowledge extraction.

Knowledge discovery is a process that extracts implicit, potentially useful or previously unknown information from the data. The knowledge discovery process is described as follows:

Data comes from variety of sources is integrated into a single data store called Data warehouse/Data mart . The data stored in Data warehouse/Data mart is called as target data.

- The target Data is then pre-processed and transformed into standard format.
- The data mining algorithms process the data to the output in form of patterns or rules.
- Then those patterns and rules are interpreted to new or useful knowledge or information.

4. DATA MINING PROCESS

Data mining process consists of:

4.1. Classification

Classification is perhaps the most basic form of data analysis. The recipient of an offer can respond or not respond. An applicant for a loan can repay on time, repay late or declare bankruptcy. A credit card transaction can be normal or fraudulent. A packet of data traveling on a network can be benign or threatening. A bus in a fleet can be available for service or unavailable. The victim of an illness can be recovered, still ill, or deceased. A common task in data mining is to examine data where the classification is unknown or will occur in the future, with the goal of predicting what that classification is or will be. Similar data where the classification is known are used to develop rules, which are then applied to the data with the unknown classification.

4.2. Predictions

Prediction is similar to classification, except we are trying to predict the value of a numerical variable (e.g., amount of purchase), rather than a class (e.g. purchaser or non-purchaser).

4.3. Association Rules

Large databases of customer transactions lend themselves naturally to the analysis of associations among items purchased, or "what goes with what." Association rules or affinity analysis can then be used in a variety of ways. For example, grocery stores can use such information after a customer's purchases have all been scanned to print discount coupons, where the items being discounted are determined by mapping the customer's purchases onto the association rules. Online merchants such as Amazon.com and Net°ix.com use these methods as the heart of a "recommender" system that suggests new purchases to customers.

4.4. Predictive Analytics

Classification, prediction, and to some extent affinity analysis, constitute the analytical methods employed in "predictive analytics.

4.5. Data Reduction

Sensible data analysis often requires distillation of complex data into simpler data. Rather than dealing with thousands of product types, an analyst might wish to group them into a smaller number of groups. This process of consolidating a large number of variables (or cases) into a smaller set is termed data reduction.

4.6. Data Exploration

This stage usually starts with data preparation which may involve cleaning data, data transformations, selecting subsets of records and in case of data sets with large numbers of variables "fields" performing some preliminary feature selection operations to bring the number of variables to a manageable range (depending on the statistical methods which are being considered). Then, depending on the nature of the analytic problem, this first stage of the process of data mining may involve anywhere between a simple choice of straightforward predictors for a regression model, to elaborate exploratory analyses using a wide variety of graphical and statistical methods in order to identify the most relevant variables and determine the complexity and the general nature of models that can be taken into account in the next stage. Unless our data project is very narrowly focused on answering a specific question determined in advance (in which case it has drifted more into the realm of statistical analysis than of data mining),an essential part of the job is to review and examine the data to see what messages they hold, much as a detective might survey a crime scene. Here, full understanding of the data may require a reduction in its scale or dimension to allow us, to see the forest without getting lost in the trees. Similar variables (i.e. variables that supply similar information) might be aggregated into a single variable incorporating all the similar variables. Analogously, records might be aggregated into groups of similar records.

4.7. Clustering

Clustering, which is also known as Exploratory Data Analysis (EDA) is a division of data into groups of similar objects. Each group, called cluster, consists of objects that are similar among themselves and dissimilar from objects of other groups.[14]From a data mining perspective, clustering is unsupervised discovery of a hidden data concept. This approach is used in those situations where a training set of pre-classified records is unavailable. In other words, this technique has the advantage of uncovering unanticipated trends, correlations, or patterns, and no assumptions are made about the structure of the data. The management of customers 'relationships is an example of using this approach.

4.8. Data Visualization

Another technique for exploring data to see what information they hold is through graphical analysis. This includes looking at each variable separately as well as looking at relationships between variables. For numeric variables we use histograms and boxplots to learn about the distribution of their values, to detect outliers (extreme observations), and to find other information that is relevant to the analysis task. Similarly, for categorical variables we use bar charts and pie charts. We can also look at scatter plots of pairs of numeric variables to learn about possible relationships, the type of relationship, and again, to detect outliers.

4.9. Others

Another technique, data mining is the process of exploring and analyzing large quantities of data to get meaningful information and make discoveries by the patterns generated in these data. The data mining processes consist of:

(a) Defining the object of the research,

(b) Identifying the data to be analyzed,

(c) Extracting and 'cleaning' the data,

(d) Using the appropriate analysis tools,

(e) Making discoveries from the patterns that arise from this process, and

(f) Analyzing these patterns and generating reports.

5. DATA MINING TOOLS & TYPES

Different types of similar data mining tools can be found. The typical characteristics of these types are explained in this section.

5.1. Data mining suites (DMS)

DMS focus largely on data mining and include numerous methods. They support feature tables and time series, while additional tools for text mining are sometime available. The application focus is wide and not restricted to a special application field, such as business applications however, coupling to business solutions, import and export of models, reporting, and a variety of different platforms are nonetheless supported.

5.2. Business intelligence packages (BIs)

BIs have no special focus to data mining, but include basic data mining functionality, especially for statistical methods in business applications. BIs are often restricted to feature tables and time series, large feature tables are supported. They have a highly developed reporting functionality and good support for education, handling, and adaptation to the workflows of the customer.

5.3. Mathematical packages (MATs)

MATs have no special focus on data mining, but provide a large and extendable set of algorithms and visualization routines. They support feature tables, time series, and have at least import formats for images. The user interaction often requires programming skills in a scripting language. MATs are attractive to users in algorithm development and applied research because data mining algorithms can be rapidly implemented, mostly in the form of extensions (EXT) and research prototypes (RES).

5.4. Integration packages (INT)

INTs are extendable bundles of many different open source algorithms, either as stand-alone software (mostly based on Java; as KNIME, the GUI-version of WEKA,KEEL, and TANAGRA) or as a kind of larger extension package for tools from the MAT type.

5.5. EXT

EXT are smaller add-ons for other tools such as Excel, Matlab, R, and so forth, with limited but quite useful functionality. Here, only a few data mining algorithms are implemented such as artificial neural networks for Excel (Forecaster XL and XLMiner) or MATLAB.

Table 5.1. Data Mining Tools

S. No.	*Tool Name*	*Type*	*Remarks*
1.	SAS Enterprise Miner	DMS	One of the world's leading tools, enterprise oriented
2.	R	MAT	Complete statistical suit, script based, GNU-GPL
3.	Rapid Miner	DMS	Formerly YALE, more than 1000 algorithms and operators for data mining, text mining, web mining, time series analysis and forecasting, audio mining, image

			mining, predictive analytics, ETL, reporting, integrates Weka and R and Hadoop.
4.	SPSS Clementine	DMS	Former clementine, now in cooperation with IBM, Predictive Analytics Software (PASW) SPSS is an IBM company since 2009.

6. FUNCTIONS OF DATA MINING

Data mining has two main types of functions, which are descriptive mining and predictive mining.

5.1. Descriptive mining or discovery mining

The data mining process where useful information is extracted from the databases or, the discovery of potential knowledge from the databases.

5.2. Predictive mining

Data mining process that involves using machine learning to predict the unknown, or to obtain the future values of certain variables of interest from the data in the database or repositories.

The data mining system utilizes the data collection in an organization's data repositories that is, legacy systems, databases, files, etc., which are in different format and structure. Therefore, it is important that the data is formatted and structured to suit the data mining activities to produce significant results.

7. ELEMENTS OF DATA MINING

Data mining consists of five major elements, such as:

1. Extract, transform, and load transaction data onto the data warehouse system.
2. Store and manage the data in a multidimensional database system.
3. Provide data access to business analysts and information technology professionals.

4. Analyze the data by application software.
5. Present the data in a useful format, such as a graph or table.

8. LEVELS OF DATA MINING

Different levels of data mining analysis are available:

8.1. Artificial neural networks

Non-linear predictive models that learn through training and resemble biological neural networks in structure.

8.2. Genetic algorithms

Optimization techniques that use process such as genetic combination, mutation, and natural selection in a design based on the concepts of natural evolution.

8.3. Decision trees

Tree-shaped structures that represent sets of decisions. These decisions generate rules for the classification of a dataset. Specific decision tree methods include Classification and Regression Trees (CART) and Chi Square Automatic Interaction Detection (CHAID). CART and CHAID are decision tree techniques used for classification of a dataset. They provide a set of rules that you can apply to a new (unclassified) dataset to predict which records will have a given outcome. CART segments a dataset by creating 2-way splits while CHAID segments using chi square tests to create multi-way splits. CART typically requires less data preparation than CHAID.

8.4. Nearest neighbour method

A technique that classifies each record in a dataset based on a combination of the classes of the *k* record(s) most similar to it in a historical dataset (where *k*1). Sometimes called the *k*-nearest neighbour technique.

8.5. Rule induction

The extraction of useful if-then rules from data based on statistical significance.

8.6. Visualization

The visual interpretation of complex relationships in multidimensional data. Graphics tools are used to illustrate data relationships.

9. DATA MINING IN LIBRARIES AND INFORMATION CENTRES

Library is a repository where information is acquired to process, retrieve and disseminate to the right users at the right time. The library of today selects, collects and also preserves. Simultaneously, it meets the demands of varying tastes of digital environment etc. Most large commercial organizations have dedicated in-house library operations, as do schools, non-governmental organizations, as well as local, state, and central governments. With the increasing use of the Internet and the World Wide Web, digital libraries have proliferate, and these serve a huge variety of different user audiences, such as, people interested in health and medicine, science and technology, industry and world news, law, and business. With this expanded view of libraries, two key insights arise. First, libraries are nearly always embedded within larger institutions. Corporate libraries serve their corporations, academic libraries serve their universities/college/schools, and public libraries serve the general public. Second, libraries play an important role within their institutions as repositories and providers of information resources. In the provider role, libraries represent in miniature the intellectual, learning, and knowledge management activities of the people who comprise the institution.

One of the approaches of the libraries' management was to host their own library website that would provide information about their collections and services to their patrons, within and outside the premises of the library[1]. The libraries' websites should be able to provide its patrons expedite access to the information they seek; help to locate the answers required quickly; and at the same time, promote the awareness of their library to the public[4]. The implementation of the libraries' websites and the use of new IT has, indirectly, forced librarians to become more computer literate and to acquire knowledge about internet technologies which are used to plan, design and implement the services required by their patrons.

Strategic information, previously not easily available, has been facilitated with the advent of a new paradigm in IT called Data mining. The libraries require strategic information to improve the services they provide, as a result, libraries should implement data mining systems to obtain the required information. Data mining is the process of extracting valuable information from large amounts of data. The goal of data mining is processing knowledge from data, starting from raw data, through pre-processing, and ending with knowledge and to know where authors can see data mining we need to show the below diagram:

9.1. Data Mining for Library Services

Data mining can be used to improve the library services in the followingways.

9.1.1. Collection and Borrowing Activities

Library documents collection and kindred materials is a major and important function of a library. Collection development, an important function of the library, should be based on such policies and programs as would:(a) enable the library regularly to receive the books, periodicals, reports, memoranda, standards, specifications, etc., published all over the world as quickly as possible; and (b) facilitate timely access to the users of the original documents required and also enable them to be continuously aware and knowledgeable about the developments in their respective areas of interest. Trends and patterns of borrowing of resources and materials could be provided by the data mining system. For example, the type of materials being borrowed in relation to the demographics of the clients would enable the libraries' to provide or increase the popular materials or resources for their clients.

Before a library obtains new information resources (e.g., books, databases, reference tools, electronic access, etc.), a librarian assesses the needs of the existing collection in light of available and upcoming publications. Next, acquisitions personnel obtain the information resources specified from this needs assessment. Once the library obtains requested new resources, cataloguing personnel either create or purchase a catalogue record for the new resource. The circulation department then makes the resource available to end-users. Depending upon the size of the library and the scope of its operations, these activities fall within the purview of one, a dozen, or possibly hundreds of different employees organized into specialized departments.

9.1.2. Catalogue search & bibliographical database

After an information resource appears in the library's collection, users locate it using catalogue search systems and bibliographic databases. Although little uniformity exists with regard to the specifics of the user interfaces for these systems, most catalogues and bibliographic databases support a standard Web browser client as the user interface. Increasingly, catalogues and databases are cross-linked, and each user's search record and traversal of links appears in log files. When users find resources that they wish to borrow, the circulation department records their selection in a database that tracks the location of each resource owned by the library. As this overview suggests, all functional processes of the library collection assessment, acquisition, cataloguing, end user searching, and circulation generate large reserves of available data that document information resource acquisition and use. Library information systems frequently use large relational databases to store user information, resource information, circulation information, and possibly bibliographic search logs.

9.1.3. Web Logs

Web logs can produce vast amounts of data, and methods for analyzing this data can be costly and difficult to implement and complex to interpret. Currently, about 60% of libraries measure remote usage of the Internet through the library's Web page or portal. Accessing the on-line catalogue and other end-user accessible databases has accounted for a large proportion of library Web site usage. Remote access must also be distinguished from within-library access for on-line databases, and libraries have been increasing their database access through public access workstations.Data mining on the webpage log files could provide patterns on what, how and when the library sites are being used. This could provide information to the librarians on how to improve their websites.

9.1.4. Clients Information

This information is useful for the libraries to improve their services by providing the required services to the right groups of clients, such as Library services, library facilities by libraries, library facilities by facility, assistive technology etc.

Library services : There are various client information available, that is, making one-on-one appointments for advice on database searching and reference enquiries, using the Ask a Librarian online service, photocopying journal articles, requesting book retrievals, requesting items from our other libraries, retrieving physical resources, booking private study rooms, and requesting lockers. These are limited in supply more lockers are also available at the University/Colleges.

Library facilities and access : You can check the facilities available in our libraries by library and by facility.

Assistive technology : There are assistive technology rooms containing specialist computer hardware and software that can help you to get course content and other materials.

Data mining can be performed on the clients' information or demographics which can produce patterns that may determine demographics of active clients, relationships between the clients and the materials demanded behaviour pattern of the clients.

9.1.5. Circulation Information

When data mining is performed on the circulation patterns of the library collection, it may provide the librarians with the knowledge of the future needs of their clients. This can guide the librarians on their planning, budgeting, purchasing of materials which are frequently used by their clients and can provide a justification for removing or archiving unused materials. For many decades libraries have provided readers' advisory services with the help of librarians who know the collection well enough to help a user choose a work similar to other works. Market analysis can provide the same function by examining circulation histories to locate related works. In addition, this information could be provided to the OPAC to allow users to see similar works to one they have selected based upon circulation histories. While it is technically possible to build a profile for users based upon their own circulation history (Amazon.com), it may be legally and ethically questionable to do this without a user's permission. Nonetheless, by obtaining and using anonymous data from a large number of users, one can obtain similar results.

9.1.6. ILS and Data Warehouses

The Integrated Library Systems and Data Warehouses. Although the system used in most parts of the library is commonly known as an Integrated Library System (ILS), very few ILS vendors facilitate access to the data generated by the system in an integrated fashion. Instead, most librarians conceptualize their system as a set of separate data sources. While a relational database stands at the heart of most ILS systems, few system vendors provide sophisticated analytical tools that would promote useful access to this raw data. Instead, vendors encourage library staff to use pre-built front ends to access their ILS databases; these front ends typically have no features that allow exploration of patterns or findings across multiple data sets. As a first step, most managers who wish to explore biblio-mining will need to work with the technical staff of their ILS vendors to gain access to the databases that underlie their system.

Once the vendor has revealed the location and format of key databases, the next step in biblio-mining is the creation of a data warehouse. The most data mining tasks, the cleaning and pre-processing of the data can absorb a significant amount of time and effort. A truly useful data warehouse requires integration methods to permit queries and joins across multiple heterogeneous data sources. Only by combining and linking different data sources can managers uncover the hidden patterns that can help understand library operations and users. After the data warehouse is set up, it can be used for not only traditional SQL-based question-answering, but also online analytical processing (OLAP) and data mining. Multidimensional analysis tools for OLAP (Cognos) would allow library managers to explore their traditional frequency based data in new ways by looking at statistics along easily changeable dimensions. The same data warehouse that supports OLAP also sets the stage for data mining. This data warehouse will lower the cost of each biblio mining project, which will improve the cost/benefit ratio for these projects. The remainder of this chapter builds on the assumption that this data warehouse is available.

9.2. Decision-making Tool for Library Management

Data mining could help the libraries with decision-making in a number of areas, such as –

9.2.1. Removal of Unused Material

Dr.S.R.Ranganathan (1988) fifth law of library science states "Library is a growing organism". This development should include weeding out of obsolete and unwanted books and adding new ones which are relevant and useful. By performing data mining on the pattern of library circulation, materials that are not in circulation could be replaced with newer edition or the materials which are not in circulation could be stored somewhere else.

9.2.2. Staff Management

Managing is the art of creating and maintenance of an internal environment in an enterprise where individuals, working together in groups, can perform efficiently and effectively towards the attainment of group goals. Human Resources Development is a process of helping employees in an organisation to acquire new skills and competence on a continuing basis. The organisation should provide facilities to the employees in a planned and systematic way to acquire and sharpen skills and capabilities to perform various tasks associated with their present and expected future roles; develop their general capabilities, discover and exploit their inner potential for their own and organisational development purposes; help bring about an organisational culture in which collaboration among sub-units is strong and contributes to the supervisor-subordinate relationships, team work and the professional well-being and pride of employees; facilitate upgrading of skills through mechanisms and instruments; and improve abilities by the introduction of strategic and operational HRD planning and execution. By performing data mining on the circulation of materials a pattern could be discovered on when and what type of services are in demand at a particular time. For example, if there is a pattern that shows there could be less renewal and borrowing of books in the morning, the librarian could be assigned to other library activities. This would ensure that the library staff is being fully utilized.

9.2.3. Purchasing of Materials

Data mining on the circulation could provide patterns on what types of books or materials are in demand and this may help the library in purchasing the 'right' materials for their clients. This information can be used to justify the purchasing of materials to the libraries' management.

9.3. Reporting and Justification

Library management, as most entities, have to provide reports and justification on decisions made. Data mining could provide the required information by following reports.

9.3.1. Library's Usage

The increases in non-book materials in the libraries today are making it complex in its processing and retrieval. In a library the ultimate objective is to satisfy every types of user, whatever their genuine needs are to be me.t For the smoothly usage of resources by the users, data mining could provide management with projections of the future trends of the library usage. This could justify the need to increase the budget or resources allocated to the library.

9.3.2. Library's Staff Justification

Library management is the process of organized activity consisting of operations and the librarian as a leader must option to the art of working through motivating others and directing them towards objectives. Data mining can produce projection on the future requirement of the library and the growth of the library. The library management can justify and increase its work force based on this report.

9.4. Data mining: expect future user needs

By looking for patterns in high-use items, librarians can better predict the demand for new items in order to determine how many copies of a work to order. To prevent inventory loss, predictive modelling can be used to look for patterns commonly associated with lost/stolen books and high user fees. Once these patterns have been discovered, appropriate policies can be put in place to reduce inventory losses. The library can also better serve their user audience by determining areas of deficiency in the collection. The reference desk and the OPAC are two sources of data that can aid in solving problems with the collection. If the topics of questions asked at the reference desk are recorded along with the perceived outcome of the interaction, then patterns can be discovered to guide librarians to areas that need attention in the collection.

10. OPEN SOURCE DATA MINING LIBRARY SOFTWARE

There are various kinds of open-source data mining library software packages, such as-

10.1. Mlpack(C++ library)

MLPACK (http://mlpack.org/) is a machine learning software library for C++.It is built on top of the Armadillo library in January 7,2015. MLPACK has an emphasis on scalability, speed, and ease-of-use. Its aim is to make machine learning possible for novice users by means of a simple, consistent API, while simultaneously exploiting C++ language features to provide maximum performance and maximum flexibility for expert users. Its intended target users are scientists and engineers.

It is open source software distributed under the BSD license, making it useful for developing both open source and proprietary software. Releases 1.0.11 and before were released under the LGPL license. The project is supported by the Georgia Institute of Technology and contributions from around the world.

10.2. Natural Language Toolkit

The Natural Language Toolkit or more commonly NLTK (www.nltk.org), is a suite of libraries and programs for symbolic and statistical natural language processing (NLP) for the Python programming language set up in September 7, 2014.It is NLTK includes graphical demonstrations and sample data. It is accompanied by a book that explains the underlying concepts behind the language processing tasks supported by the toolkit,plus a cookbook.

NLTK is intended to support research and teaching in NLP or closely related areas, including empirical linguistics, cognitive science, artificial intelligence, information retrieval, and machine learning.NLTK has been used successfully as a teaching tool, as an individual study tool, and as a platform for prototyping and building research systems.

10.3. OpenNN (Open Neural Networks Library)

OpenNN stands for Open Neural Networks Library(www.intelnics.com/opennn) is a software library written in the C++ programming language which implements neural networks. The library is open source, hosted at Source Forge and licensed under the GNU Lesser General Public License. It was formerly known as Flood.

OpenNN implements data mining methods as a bundle of functions. These can be embedded in other software tools using an application programming interface (API) for the interaction between the software tool and the predictive analytics tasks. In this regard, a graphical user interface is missing but some functions can support the integration of specific visualization tools.

OpenNN is a general purpose artificial intelligence software package, which can be used for machine learning, data mining and predictive analytics tasks in different fields. For instance, the library has been applied in the engineering, energy, or chemistry sectors.

10.4. Torch (machine learning)

Torch (www.torch.ch) is an open source deep learning library for the Lua programming language and a scientific computing framework with wide support for machine learning algorithms. It is stable released on February 18, 2015. It uses a fast scripting language LuaJIT, and an underlying C implementation.

The core package of Torch is torch. It provides a flexible N-dimensional array or Tensor, which supports basic routines for indexing, slicing, transposing, type-casting, resizing, sharing storage and cloning. This object is used by most other packages and thus forms the core object of the library. The Tensor also supports mathematical operations like max, min, sum, statistical distributions like uniform, normal and multinomial, and BLAS operations like dot product, matrix-vector multiplication, matrix-matrix multiplication, matrix-vector product and matrix product.

11. COPYRIGHT LAW IN DATA MINING

Protection of copyright in digital information environment is the major problem. The main reasons of copyright violation are expensive cost of books/journals, non-availability of books, ignorance of copyright laws etc. The violations have created a number of issues of copyright such as databases, software ,multimedia works ,internet ,data mining and downloading etc. The present copyright laws are not able to prevent piracy or infringements of right. So, the persons who want to make copies from its original version without getting permission from its owner should be punished. It is therefore necessary copyright laws should be strongly updated to stop the theft of intellectual products.

11.1. Status of Copyright Law in European Continent

As with all fields of intellectual property copyright is concerned with protecting the work of the human intellect. The domain of copyright is the protection of literary and artistic works. These include writings, music, and works of the fine arts, such as paintings and sculptures, and technology-based works such as computer programs and electronic databases.

Note that copyright protects works that is the expression of thoughts, and not ideas. Due to a lack of flexibilities in European copyright and database law, the mining of in-copyright works such as web mining without the permission of the copyright owner is not legal. Where a database is pure data in Europe there is likely to be no copyright, but database rights may exist so data mining becomes subject to regulations by the Database Directive. On the recommendation of the Hargreaves review this led to the UK government to amend its copyright law in 2014 to allows content mining as a limitation and exception. Only the second country in the world to do so after Japan, which are introduced an exception in 2009 for data mining. Though due to the restriction of the Copyright Directive, the UK exception only allows content mining for non-commercial purposes. UK copyright law also does not allow this provision to be overridden by contractual terms and conditions. The European Commission facilitated stakeholder discussion on text and data mining in 2013, under the title of Licenses for Europe. The focus on the solution to this legal issue being licenses and not limitations and exceptions led to representatives of universities, researchers, libraries, civil society groups and open access publishers to leave the stakeholder dialogue in May 2013.

11.2. Status of Copyright Law in the American Continent

The Copyright Act of 1790 was the first federal copyright act to be instituted in the United States, though most of the states had passed various legislation securing copyrights in the years immediately following the Revolutionary War. The stated object of the act was the "*encouragement of learning,*" and it achieved this by securing authors the "sole right and liberty of printing, reprinting, publishing and vending" the copies of their "maps, charts, and books" for a term of 14 years, with the right to renew for one additional 14 year term should the copyright holder still be alive. By contrast to Europe, the flexible nature of US copyright law and in particular fair use means that content mining in America, as well as other fair use countries such as Israel, Taiwan and South Korea is viewed as being legal. As content mining is transformative, that is it does not supplant the original work, it is viewed as being lawful under fair use. For example as part of the Google Book settlement the presiding judge on the case ruled that Google's digitization project of in-copyright books was lawful, in part because of the transformative uses that the digitization project displayed - one being text and data mining.

12. CONCLUSION

The information explosion is a serious challenge for current information institutions. On the other hand, data mining, which is the search for valuable information in large volumes of data, is one of the solutions to face this challenge. In the past several years, data mining has made a significant contribution to the field of information science. Owing to automation of libraries, they have gathered data about their collections and users for years, but have rarely used those data for better decision-making. By taking a more active approach based on applications of data mining, data visualization, and statistics, information organizations can get a clearer picture of their information delivery and management needs. At the same time, libraries must continue to protect their users and employees from misuse of personally identifiable data records. Libraries must compete against online booksellers, downloadable audio books, and the vast supply of "free" information of varying quality from the Internet, librarians must begin to take the initiative in using their systems and data for competitive advantage and to justify continued support and funding of libraries. The process of using library data more effectively begins by discovering ways to connect the disparate sources of data most libraries create. Connecting these disparate sources in data warehouses can facilitate systematic exploration with different tools to discover behavioural patterns of the libraries primary constituencies. These patterns can help enhance the library experience for the user, can assist library management in making decisions and setting policies, and can assist the parent organizations or communities to understand information needs of their members.

Many advanced for data mining are available either as open-source software. They cover a wide range of software products, from comfortable problem-independent data mining suites, to businesss- centered data warehouses with integrated data mining capabilities, to early research prototypes for newly developed methods. In this chapter, different types of data mining tools are presented: DMS, BIs, MATs, INT, EXT, etc. They vary in many different characteristics, such as intended user groups, possible data structures, implemented tasks and methods, interaction styles, import and export capabilities, platforms and license policies are variable. Recent tools are able to handle large datasets with single features, time series, and even unstructured data like texts; however, there is a lack of powerful and generalized mining tools for multidimensional datasets such as images and videos.

This chapter also focused the open-source data mining library software packages whereas the status of copyright in European as well as American continents.

REFERENCES

1. Branscomb, A. (1986). "Law and culture in the information society". *Information Society.* Vol .4 No.4, pp.279-311.
2. Conkling; *et al.*(2001), "Engineering libraries: Building collections and delivering services". *Sci. Technol. Lib.*,Vol.19 No.3,p.208.
3. Lone, T. A. and Khan, R. A. (2014), "Data mining: competitive tool to digital library", *DESIDOC Journal of Library & Information technology*, Vol.34, No.5, pp.401-406.
4. Ha, S., Bae, S., & Park, S. (2000). Web mining for distance education. In *IEEE international conference on management of innovation and technology* (pp. 715–719).
5. Weiss, S. H., & Indurkhya, N. (1998). *Predictive Data Mining: A Practical Guide.* San Francisco, CA: Morgan Kaufmann Publishers.
6. Data Mining (2015),What is Data Mining? Available at: *www.anderson.ucla.edu*
7. Feather, J. and Sturges, P. (Eds.). (2003). *Routledge International Encyclopedia of Information and Library Science.* Routledge,p.122.
8. Hand, D., Mannila, H. & Smyth, P. (2001), *Principles of Data Mining.* Cambridge, MA:The MIT Press.
9. Berry, M. J. A. &Linoff G. S. (1997), *Data Mining Techniques.* New York: Wiley.
10. Berry, M. J. A. &Linoff, G. S. (2000), *Mastering Data Mining.* New York: Wiley.
11. Prakash, K.,Chand,P., and Gohel, U.(2004). Application of data mining in library and information services.In*2nd Convention PLANNER - 2004, Manipur Uni., Imphal, 4-5 November*,pp.169.
12. Gangurde, R. A. and Sonar, M. R. (2014), "Knowledge Extraction using Data Mining Techniques", Spvryan's International Journal of Engineering Sciences & Technology,Vol.1 No.1,pp.1-4.
13. J.W. Tukey, (1977), Exploratory data analysis (Addison-Wesley, Reading, MA).

14. D. Roussinov and J.L. Zhao, (2003),"Automatic discovery ofsimilarity relationships through Web mining", *Decision Support Systems*, Vol. 35 No.1,pp.149-166.

15. Bruxella, J.M.D., Sadhana, S. and Geetha, S. (2014). "Categorization of Data Mining Tools Based on Their Types". *International Journal of Computer Science and Mobile Computing*, Vol.3 No.3, pp.445–452.

16. Zhengxin,C.(2001),Data mining and uncertain reasoning: an integrated approach.John Wiley & Sons, Inc.,New York.

17. Wikipedia, Free Encyclopedia (2015), Data mining. Available at: http://en.wikipedia.org/wiki/Data_mining.

18. Hussain, A., & Abalkhail, A. M. (2013),"Determinants of library use, collections and services among the students of engineering: a case study of King Saud University",*Collection Building*, Vol.32 No.3,pp. 100-110.

19. Oracle and Sun Microsystems(2015), "Information technology advances in libraries",Available at:http://www.oracle.com/us/sun/index.htm

20. Gangurde, R. A. and Sonar, M. R. (2014), "Knowledge Extraction using Data Mining Techniques", *Spvryan's International Journal of Engineering Sciences & Technology*,Vol.1 No.1,pp.1-4.

21. Farlex, Free Dictionary(2015), data mining. Available at: *http://www.thefreedictionary.com/data+mining*

22. Nicholson, S. and Stanton, J. Gaining strategic advantage through bibliomining: Data mining for management decisions in corporate, special, digital, and traditional libraries. InNemati,H.andBarko,C.(Ed.)*Organizational Data Mining: Leveraging Enterprise Data Resources for Optimal Performance*, Idea Group Publishing, Hershey, PA.

23. Jorgensen, C.(2005),"The internet and public library use", in Drake, M.(Ed.), *Encyclopedia of Library and Information Science*.2nd Ed., Taylor & Francis, Georgia, USA, p.263.

24. Ranganathan,S.R.(1988),Five Laws of Library Science, UBS Publishers Distributors, Delhi.

25. Curtin, R *et al.* (2013), "MLPACK: A Scalable C++ Machine Learning Library", *Journal of Machine Learning Research*, Vol.14,pp.801-805.

26. Wikipedia, Free Encyclopedia (2015), Natural Language Toolkit. Available at : http://en.wikipedia.org/wiki/Natural_Language_Toolkit

27. Bruxella, J.M.D., Sadhana, S. and Geetha, S. (2014). "Categorization of Data Mining Tools Based on Their Types". *International Journal of Computer Science and Mobile Computing*, Vol. 3 No. 3, pp. 445–452.

28. Wikipedia, Free Encyclopedia (2015), Torch (machine learning). Available at:http://en.wikipedia.org/wiki/Torch_(machine learning).

29. Copyright in European continent (2015), "Text and Data Mining: Its importance and the need for change in Europe". Association of European. Available at: http://libereurope.eu/blog/2013/04/25/text-and-data-mining-its-importance-and-the-need-for-change-in-europe/

30. Copyright in American continents (2015), "Judge grants summary judgment in favor of Google Books - a fair use victory". Lexology.com. Antonelli Law Ltd. Available at:http://www.lexology.com/library/detail.aspx?g=a18c5b92-5a20-4d1d-a098-a3095046a88e

PART-IV
Content Management

9

Artificial Intelligence (AI): A Catalyst to Content Management Systems (CMS)

Sreelatha K

1.0. INTRODUCTION

Artificial intelligence is generally the computing technologies pre-programmed and works like human intelligence such as reasoning, learning, adaptation, sensory understanding and interaction. AI solves specific problems or tasks for which it is designed. The use of machine learning and AI technologies are used to perform tasks that are traditionally done by humans. The tasks which require minimum level of cognitive thinking, where a human performs the task in less than a second can be automated with simple AI techniques. Examples are face recognition, topic of a text, predicting the time to complete a task etc.

* Professional Assistant, CHMK Library, University of Calicut.

In our data world, it is finding difficult to classify contents which were manually done with some categorization, and such filing cannot be feasible for large amount of data. Automating and simplifying the process AI is playing an important role. Machine learning, natural language processing and other AI based technologies assist in classification and retrieving it in personalized manner. The application of artificial intelligence technologies can enhance the content management systems. Searching the contents can be made more easier and can maintain the precision in the results.

1.1. Content Management

The origin of content management was in BC 300 to AD 720s, where the knowledge was preserved in papyrus rolls and clay tablets in Alexandria library. Thus, the first initiators of content management were librarians. The business catch up gradually around the world and the 20th century saw great number of scientists who researched on content management like, S R Ranganathan, Paul Otlet , Melwil Dewey and many others to name. Content management became a challenge with the introduction of internet and www. Content management is defined as "a set of processes and technologies that supports the collection, managing and publishing of information in any form or medium when stored and accessed via computer. This information may be more specifically referred to as digital content or simply as content".

There are seven stages in content management like,

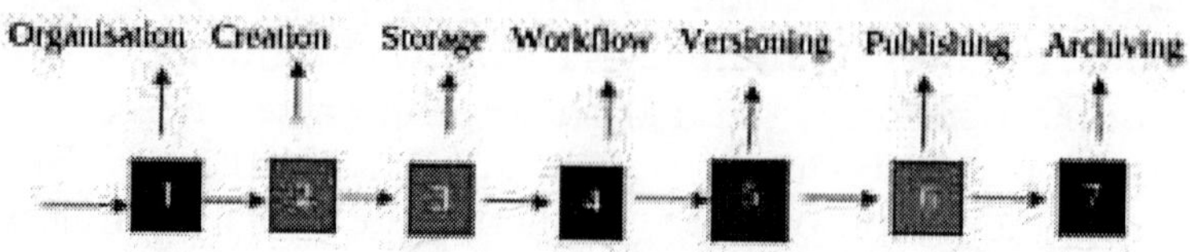

Fig. 1. Process of CMS

The flooding of information and knowledge became uncontrollable and tracking of content was a puzzle. The web content was stored in HTML and XML scripts and not easy to understand for a lay man. These difficulties laid to the designing of content management systems.

1.2. Content Management Systems

A content management system (CMS) is a software package which facilitates to automate the seven process of content management and effectively manage the content archived. A CMS runs on a server with multiuser accessibility which interacts with the content of the repository. The popular software choices are Drupal, Jhoomla and WordPress for effective content management. WordPress is an open source blog software package that works exceptionally well as content management system, a blog system, or a traditional website. Drupal is a free software package that allows anyone to easily publish, manage and organize a wide variety of content on a website. Joomla is a content management system, which enables us to build Web sites and powerful online applications. All these software's have user friendly interfaces for creating repository, editing, publishing and archiving. The front end interfaces for the user are made simple to search and retrieve contents. The web content management system works in the following way:

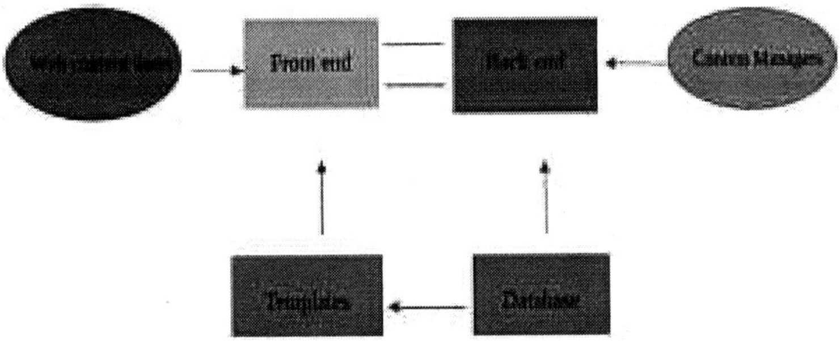

Fig. 2. Working of Web CMS and User interface

The CMS discussed here is intended to manage

digital content on web. A CMS has two parts namely Server (database) and client (user interface) parts.

2.0. ARTIFICIAL INTELLIGENCE

Human beings are distinguished from other animals because of their intelligence. They are now craving for creating machines, robots and software which can think and act faster than human beings. Artificial intelligence is a branch of computer science that aims to create intelligent machines. It has become an essential part of the technology industry. The original roots and ideas of that must be searched for philosophy, linguistics, mathematics, neurology and physiology, branches and sub branches and it's different application through computer and engineering, biology, medicine, communication and plenty of other fields. For better explanation of artificial intelligence, it is worthwhile to say it is possible for man to produce intelligence like him. Research associated with artificial intelligence is highly technical and specialized. The core problems of artificial intelligence include programming computers for certain traits such as:

- Knowledge
- Reasoning
- Problem solving
- Perception
- Learning
- Planning
- Ability to manipulate and move objects

Artificial intelligence (AI) is an area of computer science that emphasizes the creation of intelligent machines that work and reacts like humans. Some of the activities computers with artificial intelligence are designed to include:

- Speech recognition

- Learning
- Planning
- Problem solving

Knowledge engineering is a core part of AI research. Machines can often act and react like humans only if they have abundant information relating to the world. Artificial intelligence must have access to objects, categories, properties and relations between all of them to implement knowledge engineering. Initiating common sense, reasoning and problem-solving power in machines is a difficult and tedious task.

Machine learning is also a core part of AI. Learning without any kind of supervision requires an ability to identify patterns in streams of inputs, whereas learning with adequate supervision involves classification and numerical regressions. Classification determines the category an object belongs to, and regression deals with obtaining a set of numerical input or output examples, and discovers functions enabling the generation of suitable outputs from respective inputs. Mathematical analysis of machine learning algorithms and their performance is a well-defined branch of theoretical computer science often referred to as computational learning theory.

Machine perception deals with the capability to use sensory inputs to deduce the different aspects of the world, while computer vision is the power to analyze visual inputs with a few sub-problems such as facial, object and gesture recognition. Robotics is also a major field related to AI. Robots require intelligence to handle tasks such as object manipulation and navigation, along with sub-problems of localization, motion planning and mapping.

2.1. AI and CMS

AI is not a threat to CMS it can challenge CMS to perform better. It can enhance the features, look and feel of a content management system. Most of the Content

Service Providers have started integrating AI techniques to provide better search results. EBSCO Discovery, Vu Find , Google Vision etc are examples of such adaptations. The integration of additional tools will allow enterprise users to create and adapt models to their specific needs in an intelligent and highly-automated manner. We have seen AI has shown magic like self driving cars, sensors to monitor patients, drons and many others. The CMS is the area where AI is least utilised. AI is being used in content management to analyze past and current consumer behavior, to help determine priorities, to predict which customers are likely to buy particular products or services and the best way to reach and engage them. Online stores like Flipkart, Amazon, Ebay etc., are adopting this technique to sell their products. Similarly in CMS users can be analysed , their needs and area of interest can be known by applying AI based on search from particular system or based on IP address they can be given the content of their interest.

2.2. Where AI can be applied

The arrival of AI is a key inflection point in the ongoing journey to revolutionize Content Services. The market is poised for additional advances with AI, not just as a tool for metadata extraction, but also as a key technology for automating decision-making and personalizing content delivery. AI is helping Content Service Providers scale to new heights, with the first object benchmark in the industry on the horizon and potentially new applications that will entirely change how digital assets are created, managed, and distributed. The various areas where AI can be introduced are :

- Searching
- Content generation
- Website designing
- Content promotion

Searching

AI technologies can be used in content management systems to interpret the query and give better answers. RankBrain is an example of AI used by Google to interpret and process queries and rank web pages.

Content generation

There are powerful AI technologies which can convert data into insightful narratives at a good speed and scale. These Natural Language Generators can be utilised for content generation. Wordsmith is an example for NLG Platform which helps in transforming data and publishing.

Website designing

AI powered web designer programs can design your website as per your choice of theme, layout and color scheme. The Grid is such a program where it AI , Molly, is the one optimizing, arranging and designing the website according to one's theme, preference, and content. WixADI, Firedrop and Adobe Sensei are other examples.

CONCLUSION

Website developers will be able to prepare a beautiful website if he has good ability to manage the content. Web Content Management system allows developer to publish content to the web without having advanced knowledge of web technology or programming . Now, web content can include text, images, audio and video. Also a modern WCMS can also include workflow features like creating, storing, and updating of web pages.. So a mathematical approach of a function on a set can be helpful to manage content and will publish a very high standard and excellent website. Content Management System does a number of things and the reason preferred is convenience. People are able to track, monitor their content from anywhere, no matter what system or OS they are using. One of the problems of CMS was their inability to organize and index content. They were not smart enough to identify people, places and other references mentioned in a document. With an AI approach, the content systems will be able to manage and group content using "text clustering" technology. Using a common machine learning technique, content management systems can identify and extract meaning so that it could be employed in a larger context. When AI would automatically tell content management systems what the documents exactly are, organizations do get a major productivity boost, cut down on errors and even increases user adoption. The adoption of AI in content management will be a revolution in the area.

REFERENCES

1. David Jones, Nuxeo (2018) "How AI Is Changing Content Management", ECM Connection , June 14. *https://www.ecmconnection.com* retrieved on 08.10.2018.
2. Manoj Kumar Srivastav and Asoke Nath (2016) "Web content management system", International Journal of Innovative Research in Advanced Engineering (IJIRAE) , Vol. 3 Issue 3, pp.51-56.
3. Mohammad ziaaddini and Aref Tahmasb (2014) "Artificial intelligence handling throughteaching and learning process and it's effect on science-based economy". International Journal on Soft Computing, Artificial Intelligence and Applications (IJSCAI), Vol.3, No. 1, pp1-7.
4. Michael Seadle, (2006) "Content management systems", Library Hi Tech, Vol. 24 Issue: 1, pp.5-7, *https://doi.org/10.1108/07378830610652068*
5. Susan Goodwin, Nancy Burford, Martha Bedard , Esther Carrigan, Gale C. Hannigan, (2006) "CMS/CMS:content management system/change management strategies", Library Hi Tech, Vol. 24 Issue: 1, pp.54-60, *https://doi.org/10.1108/07378830610652103*
6. http://www.slideshare.net/smtch/web-content-management

10

Content-Management Software: A Focus on Joomla & Drupal

Rajib Kalita*

1. CONTENT MANAGEMENT SOFTWARE (CMS)

Today we are living in the information age. Information on the web is growing tremendously, and searching on the Internet today can be compared to dragging a net across the surface of the ocean. The Internet's explosion created a new set of problems for site administrators. Producing and managing content was becoming increasingly difficult. A system was needed to manage, create, and distribute various forms of content.

A Content Management System (CMS) is a computer application that enables users to manage content in an orderly fashion. Content can include a variety of file types such as text, images, and media, which a CMS helps to create, edit, store and publish. The benefit of using a CMS, especially for website creation, is that it does not require

* Mphil Scholar, Department of Library & Information Science, Gauhati University, Assam.

an extensive knowledge of coding. Most CMS's are built on the LAMP (Linux Apache MySQL PHP) stack and are FOSS (Free Open Source Software). Every CMS now uses downloadable add-ons known as modules or extensions. Modules enable the community and other third parties to expand the capability beyond the original intent. There are many CMS like Joomla, Drupal, Mambo, SilverStripe etc.

2. JOOMLA

Joomla is a class of Open Source CMSs written in PHP scripting language and uses MySQL database for the backend. Compared to other CMSs Joomla is fairly new and is gaining popularity among users because of many aspects, including ease of usability and extensibility. There are more than 7500 extensions and modules available to enhance the functionality of the core Joomla package. Joomla can be installed and run on Linux, Windows or Macintosh OS. It is distributed under GNU GPL (General Public License) and is free to use.

Joomla is used for:

- Corporate websites or portals, intranets and extranets.
- Small business websites.
- Online magazines, newspapers, and publications.
- E-commerce and online reservations.
- Government, non-profit and organizational websites.
- Community-based, school and church websites or portals.
- Personal or family homepages.

2.1. History of Joomla

Joomla was started in 2005 as Mambo fork. Mambo (formerly named Mambo Open Source or MOS) was a free software/open source content management system (CMS) for creating and managing websites through a simple web interface. Its last release was in 2008, by which time all of the developers had left for forks of the project, mainly Joomla and MiaCMS.

2.2. Core Features of Joomla

2.2.1. Essentials

- *Multilingual* : It is available in more than 70 languages.
- *Flexible* : Make a blog, business website, intranet, community website. From the simplest to the most complex website.
- *Free for all* : Joomla is free to use under GPL(General Public License).
- *Extendable* : Over 7,500 extensions are available to extend your website and broaden its functionality.
- *User Management (ACL)* : ACL stands for Access Control List, it allows you to manage the users of your site, and different groups.
- *Menu management* : Create as many menus and menu items as you need.
- Search Engine Friendly

2.2.2. Design features

- *Template override* : Achieve superior custom designs.
- *Jlayouts* : Allows you to render HTML from objects/ arrays of data.
- *Template assignment* : Assign specific templates to specific pages.
- *Responsive* : Joomla uses Bootstrap for perfect responsive designs.
- *Do more with Less* : Joomla features LESS CSS.
- *Template frameworks* : Use external template frameworks or template clubs.
- *Create your own* : You're able to create your own

template. The only limit is your imagination.

2.2.3. Content editing & publishing:

- *Publishing tools* : Choose when articles are published.
- *WYSIWYG editor* : Edit content without any knowledge of code.
- *Content versioning* : You will never again lose a previous important version of your article and other changes on your site.
- *Article management* : Add, manage and organize your articles.
- *Editor buttons* : Add extra functions to your content in 1 click.
- *Media manager* : A tool to upload and maintain images and other files.
- *Categories* : Be able to create categories with nesting and no limits on depth.

2.2.4. Core functionalities

- *Redirect* : Easily redirect URLs when needed.
- *Banners* : Monetize your website by adding banners or ads.
- *Contacts* : Add several contacts, departments and contact forms.
- *Tags* : When categorization is not enough to structure your content.
- *Syndication* : Create a RSS feed from your content.
- *News feed* : Show an external news feed on your website.
- *Custom fields* : 15 different field types to add to articles, users, and contacts.
- *Search* : Visitors will be able to quickly and easily find the appropriate information.

2.2.5. CMS Management

- *Easy core update* : Keep your Joomla up to date with 1 click.
- *Easy extensions update* : Keep your extensions up to date easy and fast.
- *Install from web* : Install extensions without leaving your backend.
- *User registration* : Allow visitors to register and gain access to additional resources.

2.2.6. Global and professional support

- *Extended documentation* : A complete wiki about Joomla
- *Integrated help system* : Joomla has an in-app contextual help system.
- *Helpful forum* : Our worldwide community of world class developers and business consultants actively help at no cost.
- *Professional service providers* : Who can help build & maintain your Joomla project.

2.3. Installation Process of Joomla

Joomla's installer is large and complex. Installer quality is very high, and has a professional fit and finish, while being easy to navigate. Firstly, we have to download the file form (https://downloads.joomla.org/). All options are presented on the screen, but the amount of options may be overwhelming. The script prompts the user to input the site URL, administrator email, MySQL account details, and a few other basic settings. Once the installer has the required information, it creates the tables. It offers a choice to populate the database with the default values, or migrate from a previous site or version. Joomla commits file system modifications through a FTP layer to enable advanced manipulations not available in PHP. If the FTP layer cannot be configured, the installer will fail and the user must complete a manual installation. While testing the installer, the FTP layer configuration failed and a manual installation had to be completed.. The manual installation was easy, but may not be simple enough for users without technical knowledge of the LAMP (Linux Apache MySQL PHP) stack. In the test case, manual installation was quicker than using the installation script. Step one creates the database using the included SQL files. Next, edit the configuration file to reflect the database connection details and administration panel password. During test case, the manual installation successfully configured the FTP layer without error. After editing the configuration file, log into the administration panel and continue setting up the system.

2.4. Joomla Project & Its Organizational Departments

The Joomla Project is governed by the Board of Directors of Open Source Matters, Inc., a not-for-profit created to provide organization, legal, and financial support to the Joomla Project. This leadership team nurtures all critical aspects of the Joomla Project to ensure its continued existence, relevance, and integrity. Open Source Matters provides the necessary foundation for the Joomla Project to receive donations, develop partnerships, retain copyrights and trademarks, and protect the individual contributors from unnecessary legal exposure.

The Joomla Project is organized into many Departments. These groups utilize the wealth of knowledge our community provides. Each of these groups focuses on a specific aspect of Joomla essential to the project's growth and development. Each department has a leadership team and together they form the Board of Directors. Hundreds of volunteers participate in the teams forming Joomla Departments.

2.5. Joomla.Com & Joomla.org

Joomla.com is the newest Joomla service that allows

you to build and maintain a completely free website. The site building software you will be using as part of the service is a slightly modified version of Joomla CMS. The website you create as part of the service will be hosted for free on the special Joomla.com hosting platform for an unlimited amount of time.

Joomla.org is the website of the great community behind Joomla CMS. On this website you can download the full version of Joomla CMS, find a detailed documentation on how to use it, get help from fellow users in the community support forums, read the project news, learn about the community events and even get involved in this amazing project.

3. DRUPAL

Drupal is a open source, cross platform content management software developed in the year 2000. Dries Buytaert is recognized as the original author of Drupal. According to Web Technology Survey (Web Technology Survey, 2017) Drupal is currently used in 2.3% of websites of entire world wide web making it the 3rd most popular CMS after Wordpress and Jhoomla. The latest stable version of Drupal is 8.4.2, which was recently released in 3rd November 2017.

The standard release of Drupal, known as Drupal core, contains basic features common to content-management systems. These include user account registration and maintenance, menu management, RSS feeds, taxonomy, page layout customization, and system administration. The Drupal core installation can serve as a simple Web site, a single- or multi-user blog, an Internet forum, or a community Web site providing for user-generated content.

3.1. System requirements for Drupal

Drupal is a cross platform CMS and is developed using PHP. Therefore running Drupal requires a web server with PHP support (like Apache). Eventhough the recommended database server is MySQL, Drupal 7 onwards support for Maria DB or Percona server is also available. As CSS is the recommended styling from HTML 5 onwards therefore any browser with CSS and Java script support is sufficient for using Drupal.

System requirements for Drupal

Disk space : A minimum installation requires 15 Megabytes. 60 MB is needed for a website with many contributed modules and themes installed. Keep in mind you need much more for the database, files uploaded by the users, media, backups and other files.

Web server : Apache, Nginx, Microsoft IIS or any other web server with proper PHP support.

Database : MySQL 5.0.15/MariaDB 5.1.44/Percona Server 5.1.70 or higher with PDO,PostgreSQL 8.3 or higher with PDO,SQLite 3.3.7 or higherMicrosoft SQL Server and Oracle are supported by additional modules

PHP : PHP 5.2.5 or higher (5.4 or higher recommended).

Browser : Internet Explorer 6.x and later, Microsoft Edge, Firefox 5.x and later, Opera 12 and later Safari 5.x and later, Google Chrome.

Examples of Major organizations website built using Drupal in national and international level are - British Broadcasting Centre (BBC), Department of Agriculture and Food Australia, MyGov.in, IIT- Bombay, Jhonson and Jhonson, HCL, Infosys, Oxford university.

4. CONCLUSION

Organization can use open source CMS to manage their contents effectively and efficiently with the features like personalization and web administrative functions. While choosing best suitable open source CMS for the organization one has to study it in detail. Analysis of various features of open source CMS can often enhance decision making. A stable, cost effective, flexible CMS which fulfills the organizational needs is an ideal choice. Open source CMS facilitate user to control overall content management solution. It provides freedom to program custom modules according to the needs. Joomla is a class of Open Source CMSs written in PHP scripting language and uses MySQL database for the backend. Compared to other CMSs Joomla is fairly new and is gaining popularity among users because of many aspects, including ease of usability and extensibility. Joomla CMS is very good for the learners who want to develop a website. Hundreds of developers have been improving Joomla since the first version was released in 2005. This immense effort has made Joomla very popular, easy to use, stable and secure. Joomla has thousands of free extensions and templates allowing you to customize your site to fit your specific needs. Drupal is a cross platform CMS and is developed using PHP. Therefore running Drupal requires a web server with PHP support (like Apache). Even though the recommended database server is MySQL, Drupal 7 onwards support for MariaDB or Percona server is also available. Drupal is released under the GPL, version 2. Anyone can download, reuse, modify, and distribute it. If you distribute derivative work (modules, themes, etc), the same terms have to be applied.

REFERENCES

1. Drupal. (2017). *Organizations Using Drupal.* Retrieved from Drupal: https://www.drupal.org/organizations.
2. Drupal Modules. (2017). *Drupal community.* Retrieved from Drupal: http://www.drupal.org/communit.
3. Giri, Kaushal K and Nirgude, Kirti R "Open Source Content Management Software : A Comparative Analysis" (paper presented at the 7th International CALBER-2009, Puducherry. Feb 25-27, 2009)184- 193.
4. Joomla Available at http://en.wikipedia.org/ wiki/Joomla (Accessed on 11/11/17)

5. Joomla Available at http://www.joomla.org/ (Accessed on 11/11/17)
6. Joomla Demo Available at http:// demo.joomla.org/ (Accessed on (12/11/17)
7. Joomla downloads Available at http:// sourceforge.net/ projects/joomla/ (Accessed on 12/11/17)
8. Web Technology Survey. (2017). *Usage of content management systems for websites.* Retrieved from Web Technology survey: https://w3techs.com/technologies/ overview/content_management/all

PART-V

ICT Initiatives and Repositories

11

Governmental Level ICT Initiatives in Kerala: An Overview

Dr. Mehaboobullah.K

1. INTRODUCTION

Kerala, one of the federal states of India, is a region known for its high levels of achievements in education, healthcare and social justice. Kerala, known far and wide as 'God's own Country', is a unique state that achieved many distinctions of all-round improvements in the social sector. Despite low per-captia income, the state's achievements in literacy, education, health, etc. are comparable to some of the developed countries.

In line with global trends, the government of Kerala formulated an Information Technology (IT) policy in the year 1998. The policy aims at increase the application of IT in all walks of life, encasing the IT industry base, creating a robust state information infrastructure and creating human resources for. The Government of Kerala

* Reference Assistant, University of Kerala, Thiruvananthapuram, Kerala.

has a comprehensive view of Information and Communication Technologies as the vehicle for transforming Kerala into a knowledge-based, economically vibrant, democratic state where the benefits of information should reach every single citizen of the State. In order to materialise these objectives the State Government has initiated a number of measures.

2. MAJOR ICT INITIATIVES IN KERALA

Majority of the government services have been transformed into the e- mode by this time. It is the Kerala State IT Mission, and autonomous nodal IT implementation agency which provides managerial support to various e- governance initiatives of the Department of Information Technology of the Government of Kerala. The major e-governance initiatives in the State are the following:

2.1. Akshaya

The Akshaya initiative was introduced to make at least one person from each family in the e- literate. In addition, the development of entrepreneurship is also coming under the domain of Akshaya project. This project is implemented in Public-Private Partnership model. The Akshaya project had its pilot implementation in Malappuram District in 2002. In 2004, Akshaya e- pay project was introduced as an online system, for the collection of various utility bills and fees. Through Akshaya e- pay, the citizens can remit their bills and dues to the government. Eventhough the Akshaya e- literacy programme was unique in nature, it raised many criticisms due to its failure in the commercial sustainability.

2.2. FRIENDS (Fast, Reliable, Instant, Effective Network for Disbursement of Services)

This is a single window 'no queue' integrated remittance centre for offering the opportunity to the citizens to pay taxes and dues to the government under single roof and without extra cost. The FRIENDS centre accepts payment of the Kerala University, Local Body, Electricity Board, Water Authorities, Land Revenue, Civil Supplies, Motor Vehicles and Electrical Inspectorate etc. The Centre works all days in a week from 9 am to 7 pm. All the counters in the Centre follows a token management system for eliminating the lengthy queues and delays in remitting the payments. For the citizens who are not having good awareness with the payment procedures, there is a Help- Desk 92 at the centre. In order to record suggestions and complaints, facilities are arranged and has regular review on them. Railway reservation facilities are also now started in FRIENDS centres.

2.3. The e-District

e-District is a State Mission Mode Project under the National e-Governance Plan. e-District as a concept proposes integrated, seamless, and online delivery of citizen services at the district level through automation of work flow, backend digitization, integration and process redesign. The project aims to target aggregate services delivered at the district level and to undertake back-end computerization for enabling the delivery of citizen services through Akshaya Centres. The Government has implemented the pilot e-District project with the vision of making all Government services accessible to the common man in his locality, through Akshaya centres and to ensure efficiency, transparency & reliability of such services.

Started in 2008, the pilot phase of the project was implementing in Kannur and Palakkad districts. KSITM (Kerala State IT Mission) has been identified as the Implementation agency of the project. Through this KSITM is planning to issue all certificates including Digital Signature of the concerned issuing officer. Kerala State IT Mission decides to roll out the e-District project throughout Kerala and has already procured 258 numbers of laptops for 3 districts (Pathanamthitta, Kottayam and

Malappuram). It is also decided to constitute a District e-Governance Society (DeGS) in all districts for monitoring the development of e-District project under DIT guidelines. The KSITM is also planned to integrate e-Payment gateway to this project have any citizen can file the application without even visiting the CSC.

2.4. SPARK (Service and Payroll Administrative Repository for Kerala)

Service and Payroll Administrative Repository for Kerala (SPARK) is a web based G2E integrated solution for Service and Payroll Management. SPARK is an attempt to bring the payroll and finance related activities of Kerala State employees within a single application. The system has been developed with a view to cater to the Administration, Payroll and other accounts activities of Government Establishments. Each employee is allotted with a unique Permanent Employee Number (PEN) through the system.

A centralized system that helps the departments to get details of any employee immediately, achieve highest level of transparency in dealing with the employees, more consistent application of rules etc. Being a well-integrated system, the changes made through one module reflect in all related areas of activity. In the payroll side, accurate and automatic payroll processing is facilitated. It also ensures that the rules and regulations are uniformly applied to all employees thereby avoiding complaints and achieving better employee-employer relations.

Kerala State has 39 Government Departments, over 122 Field Departments and over 30000 offices spread across the nook and corner of the State. Personnel and Payroll Management System using SPARK-Service and Payroll Administrative Repository for Kerala is to be implemented in all the Government Offices across the state.

Benefits

- A centralized database of the government employees for the whole state
- Unique Permanent Employee Number for all
- Necessary Government Orders issued by Govt. of Kerala
- All reports generated in PDF format
- Offline data entry package for easy data entry

2.5. Integrated Call Centre (CCC)

Citizen Call Centre (CCC) is a single window IT enabled facility of Government that act as an intermediate between citizens and Government to interact effectively through telephone. Envisaged as a government-to-citizen (G2C) interface, the Call Centre enables the quick delivery of critical information, which is otherwise either inaccessible or difficult for the citizens to trace. The relevance of a Government/Public Call Centre is more important in the context of increased focus on e-Governance and with the implementation of the Right to Information Act 2005.

CCC is providing all the services in a 24x7 fashion and working on all calendar days except national holidays. The calls are being answered by a team of Call Centre Executives, who are highly experienced and skilled professionals.

CCC wasmade operational in 2005 in Thiruvananthapuram is now serving more than 55 Government departments, organisations and projects provides information and complaint registry services for the common people. It is receiving more than thousand numbers of calls daily and there is a knowledge bank data base of 55 Government departments/projects. In addition to general enquiry, CCC also accepts complaints as part of Hon'ble Chief Minister's *Sutharyakeralam*, Check post complaints, Akshaya, State Consumer Helpline,

Kerala Women's Helpline and Aadhaar (UID) related queries also.

KSITM is planning the enhancement of CCC with the objective to increase the services rendered to citizens and also to improve the interaction with the participating departments. The new system has been proposed to transform the existing voice based Contact Centre setup into a State of the Art Contact Centre providing such service delivery channels as email, web portal, social media, online chat, SMS, MMS, FAX etc. along with conventional voice enhanced by VoIP technologies.

2.6. e-Office File Management system (e-File)

e-Office File Management system (e-File) is a Digital Workplace Solution to automate File Management in Government offices. The e-Office project in Kerala envisions modernizing government offices and getting rid of manual paper file processing and replacing it with a digital workflow system. In the process, the government offices will be transformed to 'paperless office' gaining the immense benefits of faster decision making aided by electronic mode of communication. KSWAN(Kerala State Wide Area Network) connection is required for e-Office to work. Therefore, in case KSWAN is not available at in the department, may request a leased line from the nearest KSWAN point of presence through BSNL. e-Office recommends a 4 Mbps connection for 20-25 users.

2.7. System for Attumanal Neutral Distribution (SAND)

The SAND is an outstanding technology and it fuelled intervention of the district administration in Thrissur. This software system was created from the background of unauthorized mining of river sand in Kerala. The anti-social elements make advantages through the flourishing building construction by mining river sand in an unauthorized way.

2.8. Mobile Service Gate Way

M-Governance or Mobile Governance involves the utilization of all kinds of wireless and mobile technology services, applications and devices for Governance. M-Governance, initiated by Kerala State Government, has started with the aim to utilize the strengths of Mobile penetration in the State using the concept of "always-on" connection for the delivery of government services to common people. And there by offers various government department services through mobile phones accessible to the citizens in the field, in the street, at home or other convenient locations on a 24 X 7 basis, rather than the users having to visit government offices or log on to the internet portals to access services.

M-Governance project in Kerala is perhaps the first comprehensive project of its kind undertaken by any state in the country. The vision of m-governance project is to build or showcase solutions and applications which will be benchmarks in M-governance services across the world.

2.8.1. Out Bound Dialing Facility for KISSAN KERALA project

The Mobile Service Delivery Platform has been incorporated with the KISSAN KERALA project for providing push and pull based SMS services as well as Out Bound Dialer integration has been done for providing voice based services to Farmers in regional language (Malayalam).

KISSAN Kerala project offered the following information through mobile:

- Information on the availability of planting materials
- SMS based Weather information
- SMS based information on the availability of Livestock Farms
- Soil Information on mobile
- SMS based two-way query answering system (Ask

our Experts through mobile)

- SMS based alert for the new schemes declared by the Government
- SMS based intra Departmental information management system
- SMS based information on Krishideepam Television Program
- Access Agri Videos through your mobile
- Mobile voice based monthly crop management advise
- Voice based information service

2.8.2. Computerized Call Centre for Commercial Taxes Department

The Multi-lingual IVR based Call centre and help desk has been established for the Kerala State Commercial Taxes Department. The computerized call Centre is a fully managed Interactive Voice Response Server System. A citizen who wishes to lodge complaint or a feedback can dial a 10 digit Number and record the complaint/feedback through an interactive process. Callers will get a Unique Registration Number by SMS and Voice and also will receive alerts via SMS and Voice at various stages of the Complaint.

2.8.3. State Service Delivery Gateway (SSDG) Project

State Service Delivery Gateway (SSDG) project, formulated under the National e-Governance Plan (NeGP), is to fulfill the vision of providing easy and convenient services to the citizens through remote access primarily through Common Service Centres (CSCs). And there by enabling the State Portal by implementing the key components State Portal viz. SSDG, electronic Form (e-Forms), Application and Computing Infrastructure.

The State e-Governance Service Delivery Gateway (SSDG), a core component in e-Governance infrastructure under the NeGP can act as a standards based messaging switch and providing seamless interoperability and exchange of data across departments.

The basic components of the Facilitating Services through CSC's Enabling Implementation of State Portal, SSDG & e-Forms, project are as follows:

- State Portal including Applications & electronic - forms
- State Service Delivery Gateway (SSDG)
- Training and Manpower for SSDG, State Portal
- Gap Infrastructure at the destination offices including gaps in connectivity

2.9. e-Procurement

e-Procurement or electronic procurement is an e-infrastructure specially made for business-to-government (G2B) purchase and sale of work, goods and services using the ICT tools. Also known as supplier exchange, e-procurement is a win-win approach towards buying and selling inducing and enhancing transparency, efficiency and confidentially in procurement process through the application of PKI enabled tools. As a Global standard, a 5-10 percent of cost saving is achieved through the adoption of e-Procurement system.

Benefits of e-procurement system

- Increased transparency & trust in public procurement
- Effective utilization of funds & cost reduction
- Enhanced process efficiency & better decision making
- Faster procurement cycle
- Reduced human interface
- Anytime & anywhere bidding
- Elimination of cartel formation enabling larger participation

2.10. Common Mail Service

The Email Server project envisages one another medium of communication to Kerala Government Employees, ie Email. Email provides a better speedy communication with multi-platform support solution and it can also be implemented in a short span. The security features available with email ensures the integrity of this communication. This project aims to transmute the present Government communication to another competent level.

Each mail account will also have the facilities like calendar, address, file manager etc. This gives us the possibility of having communication round the clock with no interruption and delay. This project is designed and developed on open source software

C-DIT is the implementing agency of the project.

The project started functioning in 2009. Considering the advantages of use of e mail and the legal obligations associated with it, a set of rules and policies regarding managing e mails are approved by the Government. This is prepared based on the guidelines of Department of Administrative Reforms and Public Grievances, Government of India.

2.11. Kerala Spatial Data Infrastructure (KSDI)

Kerala Spatial Data Infrastructure (KSDI) is an Internet based Geo Spatial Data Directory for the state that allow the users to share and explore the information related to political and administrative boundaries, state geography, demography, agro and socio economy, resources, infrastructure facilities with attributes. In the future the site can also be extended to sale and purchase of data online.

Spatial datasets generated, maintained and provided by various concerned Departments of the State Government, academia, private or civil society organizations of Kerala are proposed to be made accessible through the project data clearing house mechanism.

The spatial information provided through the website will help in making appropriate decisions at the local and state-level planning, implementation of state action plans, infrastructure development, disaster management support and also business development.

Benefits of KSDI

- Bringing together geo-spatial knowledge and information under a common platform, which till date has existed as a disparate system and unknown to quite a wider section of the society, institutions, scientific community and government departments
- Gateway for various data generating agencies to share the information across various government departments, NGOs, academies, industries and scientific organisation.
- Provides spatial data dictionary and map directory for the state.
- Facilitate decision support system and helps in local level planning.
- Eventually can be used for the data sale and purchase, which can be part of the state revenue generation.

2.12. Cyber Security through CERT-K

As per the Crisis Management Plan for countering cyber attacks and cyber terrorism prepared by Government of India, States should draw up their own sectoral Crisis Management Plans and implement the same. Since there is lack of adequate expertise in Government/Government Agencies/Kerala IT Mission it emerged that there is need for setting up an ongoing permanent mechanism which would act as nodal agency for monitoring various cyber security related matters for Government of Kerala/Government Organisations.

The state government have therefore to ensure cyber security of Kerala felt the necessity for setting up of Computer Emergency Response Team-Kerala (CERT-Kerala or CERT-K) in line with CERT India (CERT-IN). The purpose of CERT-K is to coordinate security efforts and incident response for IT security problems on a state level in Kerala and to enhance the security of State Government's Communications and Information Infrastructure through proactive action and effective collaboration. CERT-K shall also oversee the implementation of crisis management plan of the Government of Kerala.

2.13. Malayalam Computing

Malayalam Computing, a project that helps the common man to get more benefits out of various Internet services like E-mail, Chat, Blog etc. It liberates him or her from the need of thinking in his or her mother tongue and communicating in a foreign language.

The main bjectives of Malayalam Computing are Strengthening Malayalam language using the possibilities provided by ICT and address the linguistic barrier which prevents the people of Kerala from taking advantage of the new technologies.

2.14. e-Jaalakam

e-Jaalakam data bank which furnishes the hyperlink and briefs the services available in around 60 government websites a women may need in her lifetime. These are arranged in a life cycle pattern from birth to death enabling access according to requirements at various stages of life. e- Jaalakam pamphlet, which compiles the URLs of more than 100 useful websites, is a guide on which relevant webpage to access for various purposes.

2.15. Kerala Infrastructure and Technology for Education (KITE)

Formerly IT@School Project, was formed in 2001-

02 to fuel ICT enabled education in the schools in the State. IT@School was transformed in to KITE in August 2017. KITE is the first SPV (Special Purpose Vehicle) Company of the Education Department of the State. KITE also became the first SPV to get funded by Kerala Infrastructure and Investment Fund Board (KIIFB), the apex body for monitoring all the projects envisaged by the Govt. The hitherto scope of General Education Sector has now been extended further with KITE being positioned to fuel ICT support to Higher Education sector also including Arts & Science, Engineering colleges and Universities.

IT@School was formed in 2001, as a Project under General Education Department, to inculcate IT activities in Higher School sections in the State. The first break through of IT@School came in 2005 when Information Technology was made a compulsory subject in Std 10. The launch of EDUSAT operations and broadband connectivity to schools commenced since then, the VICTERS channel operated by IT@School was the first Complete Educational Channel in the Country. As many as 1.50 Lakh teachers from Std 1 to 12 has been empowered with ICT skills, enabling them to transact their subjects more effectively using ICT tools.

Through the transformation to a full-fledged Company under the Government, KITE has now more scope and authority for implementing various ICT programmes, when compared to the earlier Project mode of operation. KITE has already started the implementation of Hi-Tech school programme of the Education Department, by which 45000 classrooms in 4775 schools are being made Hi-Tech, for which KIIFB has already approved a funding of Rs.493.50 Crores.

2.15.1. Hi -Tech School

The Hi-Tech school programme is a major highlight of the Public Education Rejuvenation Mission of the State

Govt, aimed at upgrading all classrooms to international standards. KITE was identified as the implementing agency for the programme, being the pioneer of ICT enabled education in the State for over a decade. The Detailed Project Report for implementing the Hi-Tech school programme for 4775 schools at a total estimated cost of Rs.493.50 Cr, prepared by KITE was approved by KIIFB, the nodal agency for monitoring all Govt projects.

Each classroom would be equipped with Laptop, Multimedia Projector, Whiteboard and Sound system. Each Hi-Tech IT Lab would feature Desktop Computers with UPS, Multifunction Printers, LCD TV and a HD Camera. Specific Security features would be installed in schools. The IT Labs and Classrooms would be connected via network through a Central server in the Lab, which would allow sharing of information. High Speed fibre based Broadband internet would be made available in all classrooms

After successfully undertaking a pilot implementation of Hi-Tech School Programme in 139 selected schools in 4 constituencies – Alappuzha, Puthukkad, Kozhikode North and Thaliparamba and also including the 7 Smart Schools, the State wide launch of the programme was inaugurated by Hon.Chief Minister on 22 January 2018 at Thiruvananthapuram.

2.15.2. Capacity Building for Teachers and Students

As part of the pilot implementation, KITE has imparted ICT based trainings to 77,194 teachers from High School, Higher Secondary, Vocational Higher Secondary and Upper Primary sections. In addition to this, as many as 52,150 students from 1990 High Schools, who are members of Little KITEs Clubs, were also trained in various domains such as Animation, Electronics, Hardware, Cyber Safety, Malayalam Computing, Web TV, Development of Mobile Apps, Programming, Robotics, E-Commerce, E-Governance, Video Documentation etc.

2.15.3. Content Development- SAMAGRA

KITE has developed SAMAGRA Resource Portal which functions as a repository of educational contents for students from class 1 to 12. Samagra features e-Resources, Textbooks and Question Banks in the form of images, videos, animations, interactive narrations and tutorials. Till date Samagra has over 20,000 digital resources, in four mediums of instruction- Malayalam, English, Tamil and Kannada. Specific content development workshops are conducted at various levels at regular intervals.

2.15.4. eWaste Management from schools

KITE had tied up with Clean Kerala Company of Govt of Kerala dispose over 1 Cr kilograms of e-Waste from over 10,000 schools and educational offices in Kerala. It has been reported that the eWaste which has been accumulated since the past two decades, eats-up huge space of IT labs, besides obstructing the lab activities in a large way. As on date over 545 Tonnes of eWaste has been disposed from 14 districts. Equipments such as Desktop Computers, CRT Monitors, Laptops, Desktop Cabinets, Drives, Printers, Projectors, UPS, Camera, Speaker System, Television, Network Components, Generators etc are being included in the eWaste category.

2.15.5. Sampoorna

Sampoorna School Management Software was initially launched by KITE in 2010 as part its eGovernance initiatives. SAMPOORNA has now been mandatory by the State Government for capturing details of all students from Std 1 to 12. The application has been developed by KITE entirely on a FOSS platform as , is a one-stop source for all details of students such as Transfer Certificate, various reports, entry forms- to name a few. Government has now directed all schools in the State including Government and Aided Schools, CBSE, ISCE, Kendriya Vidyalayas and

Recognized Un-Aided schools to capture complete details of their students only through Sampoorna. Currently different sections under Education Department as well as other agencies and departments provide the same data to schools but in different formats either online or offline, which often creates confusion at various levels. By making Sampoorna mandatory, there will only be a single form of data generated from Sampoorna which also paves way for a complete digital data collection mechanism in Education Department, eventually creating a paper-less environment.

2.15.6. VICTERS

Moving ahead with time, KITE has enhanced the educational scenario in the state to a new level by making use of EDUSAT facilities. KITE, formerly IT@School Project, was the nodal agency for EDUSAT operations in the state. EDUSAT was the dedicated satellite that India has launched exclusively for the purpose of imparting education. With the technical support from ISRO, KITE successfully implemented various activities based on EDUSAT till date. The first phase of the programme was mainly through various interactive classroom sessions, facilitated by Receive Only Terminals, provided to selected schools, which enabled valuable exchange between subject experts and students, and besides such discussions, the students are able to expand their knowledge in academic subjects as well as gain new insights at the social level.

The second phase of EDUSAT initiative was the launch of an educational channel - IT@School VICTERS (Versatile ICT Resource for Students) in 2006. Through Receive Only Terminals (ROTs) a large majority of schools in the state are able to access ViCTERS.

Moving ahead with time, KITE has enhanced the educational scenario in the state to a new level by making use of EDUSAT facilities. KITE, formerly IT@School Project, was the nodal agency for EDUSAT operations in the state. EDUSAT was the dedicated satellite that India has launched exclusively for the purpose of imparting education.

2.15.7. School Wiki

School Wiki is a unique initiative by KITE, which was launched in 2009, to foster a culture of collaborative learning among students. School Wiki currently features details of over 15,000 schools in Kerala and gives a bird's eye view on the schools' elementary data, historical references, infrastructure, renowned Alumni, School websites, School Map, Blogs, Class Magazines, supporting images and videos. It has over 30,997 articles and 13,000 users and increasing day by day. Made completely in Malayalam, SchoolWiki features educational contents made by students, teachers, alumni, and public. SchoolWiki provides a platform for students, teachers and schools to showcase their areas of excellence like no other portal.

The aim of School Wiki is to bring out collaborative data building and to generate more interest among students to learn Malayalam and to generate more contents in various subjects. Since SchoolWiki is completely made in Malayalam, it enables students from all streams to understand and learn the contents with ease. The best educational contents which are developed by students are chosen through a transparent competition and the selected resources are uploaded in the portal for the benefit of lakhs of students. The portal also enables the teachers to share their own educational contents with not only to the students of their schools, but also to many throughout the State.

SchoolWiki is envisaged as the largest comprehensive digital repository of schools- which is first of its kind in the world. The portal also acts as a resource pool to which students and teachers regularly contribute educational contents made by them. KITE has already initiated a student network titled 'Hi School Kuttikootam' in which Student School IT Co-ordinators (SSITCs) from all schools would be trained in 5 areas such as Animation and Multimedia, Hardware, Electronics, Language computing and Internet and Cyber Safety. Under language Computing, students would be given intense training on how to make use of SchoolWiki to the maximum. The shifting of the application to the new server would also help in hosting larger educational contents including videos and pictures. The Kuttikootam programme could be the largest students' IT network in the Country, and would cover 1 lakh students this year and 2 lakhs by next year. This programme would also highlight on teaching the students on the importance of language computing, thereby giving the students an opportunity to undertake different language computing programmes.

2.15.8. Modernisation of Schools and Colleges

Under the programme 1,000 Government Schools in the State of Kerala as "Centres of Excellence" under the "Public Education Rejuvenation Campaign"of theGeneral Education Department (GED) of Government of Kerala. This ambitious programme is expected to elevate these schools to high educational standards, considering the requirements of the schools over a twenty-year horizon. The school modernisation programme is proposed to be executed in a phased manner and the first phase of this programme envisions the modernisation of schools in the following pattern.

3. CONCLUSION

In the knowledge economy of today, the state of Kerala in the Indian union which is characterized by a number of significant socio-economic, industrial and political features, might depend on its knowledge resources for its economic development. Government of

Kerala has implemented several programmes with the ultimate aim of serving citizens in a speedy and transparent manner. The state realises the importance of 'Information and Communication

Technology' as an instrument for the State's overall development. The complex and changing technology landscape, growth in internet and smart mobile phones penetration in the State, together with the proactive measures of the Government to digitally empower the citizens had helped the State to make significant strides in turning Kerala a digital state.

The achievements in E-governance front are really remarkable in kerala. In view of the quite favourable socio-economic environment of the state, particularly the abundant amount of technically qualified and skilled human resources as well as high level of social equity, the State has got excellent potential for bringing in ICT-led economic development in a balanced and equitable manner and hence to achieve rapid prosperity sans digital divide. With its continued focus on digital infrastructure and various ongoing digital initiatives, the Government's vision is to further bridge the digital divide by 2025 towards a state with digitally empowered society.

REFERENCES

1. Anand Parthasaradhy (2009), E-Governance: How Kerala Does IT: A Compendium of innovative tools and solutions crafted in the State, Kerala Information Technology Mission, Thiruvananthapuram
2. *Digital Kerala:Digitally Connected and Served State.* Kerala State Information Technology Mission,Thiruvananthapuram-Retrieved from: *www.itmission.kerala.gov.in.*
3. Government of Kerala (2007), Information Technology Policy: Towards an Inclusive Knowledge Society, Thiruvananthapuram.
4. Gupta, MP, Prabhat Kumar and Jaijit Bhattacharya: *Government Online-Opportunities and Challenges*, Tata McGraw Hill Publishing company Ltd, New Delhi.

5. Kurian, P.H. (2006), Responsible and Responsive e-Governance is the New 'Development Manthra, *Kerala Calling*, January 2006.
6. Manoj, PK, e–governance Initiatives in Kerala: the Way Ahead. *Southern Economist* ,Vol. 46, no. 21, March 2008.
7. Mohanan, P., Akshaya at a Glance, *Information Technology in Developing Countries*, Vol. 14, No.1, April 2004.
8. Nair, K.G.K & Prasad, P.N, Development through Information Technology in Developing Countries: Experiences from an Indian State", *The Electronic Journal on Information Systems in Developing Countries*, Vol. 8, No.2, Pp.1-13, 2002. (www.ejisdc.org)
9. Nissar, P,e - governance in Kerala, *Abhinav, International Monthly Refereed Journal of Research In Management & Technology* , Vol. 3, No 10 (October 2014) .
10. Niranjan Pani, Santap S. Mishra and Bijaya S. Sahu: *Modern System of Governance Good Governance vs E-Governance*, Anmol Publication Pvt. Ltd New Delhi.
11. Rajan, K. (2009), Information Communication Technology and Governance in Kerala, Kerala Economy: Trends During the Post Reform Period, *Serial Publications*, New Delhi.
12. Ramachandran Nair, K. (2007), *Governance Reforms and Development in Kerala in the Context of Globalisation* in Kameswar Chaudhary (ed.) , Globalisation, Governance Reforms and Development in India, *Sage Publications*, New Delhi, p.189
13. Sreekumar, T.T., Civil Society and The State-led Initiatives in ICTs: The Case of Kerala, *Information Technology in Developing Countries*, Vol. 12. No.3, December 2002.
14. Sukumaran Nair, P. (2007), *Professionalization of Civil Service in Kerala Problems and Prospects* in R.K. Suresh Kumar and S. Suresh Kumar (ed), Governance and Development,APH Publishing Corporation, New Delhi,.
15. www.kerala.gov.in
16. *www.akshaya.net*
17. http://www.iimahd.ernet.in/egov/ifip/jun2013
18. *http://www.lsgkerala.gov.in/egov/2012/Janasevan kendram.htm*
19. *http://www.itmission.kerala.gov.in.*
20. *http://unpan1.un.org/intradoc/groups/public/documents/apcity/unpan045526.pdf www.samagra.itschool.gov.in*

12
Overview of Institutional Repositories

*Kura Srinivas**

1. INTRODUCTION

Presently the Institutional Repository plays a vital role in the development of Higher Education systems at the University level. An institutional repository includes the digitized materials by academic, administrative course and learning materials and publications output. The authors of the learning output by the various authors deposit their publications in their Institutional Repositories. The main objective of the repositories is to create global visibility for the institutional research output to provide scholarly research of all the digitized documents like theses. Other literatures and unpublished documents are preserved in the repositories to make these unique resources observable to the user community. The five laws of Library Science constituted by Dr.S.R.Ranganthan have

* Senior Librarian, Sri Venkateshwara Engineering College, Suryapet, Telangana.

enforced the right information at the right time for the right users by creating a place for documents irrespective of the users.

The broad view of institutional repositories as a means to manage and preserve effectively an institution's knowledge base and intellectual assets results in the content of institutional repositories expanding beyond e-prints to include research data, e-learning materials and other forms of institutional intellectual outputs, which are generally not published or preserved elsewhere. Researchers, students, staff and institutions will require ongoing availability and confidence in the future accessibility of the content within the repositories. Those running institutional repositories, therefore, naturally have the responsibility to ensure this for the content they are entrusted. The challenge for digital preservation is not just the volume of data. The hardware and software used to store and access digital information are constantly upgraded and superseded. Technology obsolescence is generally regarded as the greatest technical threat to ensuring continued access to digital material.

Since the resources are generated digitally and electronically it is very easy to build a collection of any specific subject discipline or any targeted user group. It has dual role so far its functions concerned. It may be self generated knowledge-base by the Institution/ University itself on one hand, on other hand it may be the substitute model for the publication channel. With the coalition of these efforts at different demographic strata, it impacts very powerfully to the scholarly world.

An Institutional Repository consists of formally organized and managed collections of digital content generated by faculty, staff and students at an Institution. This is the collective intellectual output of an Institution, recorded in a form that can be preserved and exploited. There are the result of the vision to collect, secure and provide access to scholarly publication in a novel, digital way, mostly initiated by the Institutional library. Institutional repositories are spreading, as they have become a dispensable component for information and knowledge sharing in the scholarly world.

Institutional Repository may be defined as information systems capable of capturing, preserving and providing access to the intellectual output produced by the members of an Institution. Within the specific context of academia, an Institutional Repository may contribute to the increase of the Institution prestige and nourish the idea of an "Institutional Repository" because it manages and preserves relevant informational items that otherwise would remain scattered, unattended or inaccessible.

2. DEFINITIONS OF INSTITUTIONAL REPOSITORIES

According to Lynch (2003) "a University based Institutional Repository is a set of services that a University offers to the members of its community for the management and dissemination of digital materials created by the Institution and its community members"

Foster and Gibbons (2004) defined Institutional Repository as, "an electronic system that captures preserves and provides access to the digital work products of a community.

Raym Crow (2004) defined as Institutional Repository as a "Digital Archive of intellectual product created by the faculty, research staff, and students of an institution and accessible to end users both within and outside the institution, with few, if any barrier to access. The content is institutionally defined, scholarly, cumulative and perpetual, open and interoperable.

Chang (2003) defines an Institutional Repository as a new method for capturing, collecting, managing, disseminating and preserving scholarly works created in Digital form by the constituent members of an institution.

For the present study, the term 'Digital Libraries and Repositories' include digital collection, digital archives developed using digital library and Institutional Repository software packages.

3. THE ORIGIN OF ACADEMIC INSTITUTIONAL REPOSITORIES

Disappointment and inability created by the closed access to scholarly literature and the anomalies in journal publishing paradigm in the areas of pricing, access, copyright and host of other monopolies paved the way for open access initiatives. The core essence of open access initiatives is to make research articles in all academic fields freely available on the internet among these initiatives are the working models of open access journals and Institutional Repositories. These initiatives were directed to rescue the obliterated research world with the sole aim to provide a complimentary role by reforming the current scholarly communication impasse and to re-assert control over scholarship by the academia and to provide increased and uniform visibility of its researchers. While the open access journal models were experimented in the publisher and organizational level, institutional repositories were experimented by the educational institutions and the universities. Universities with its numerous intellectual activities in its scientific and scholarly arena and the most affected party in the closed and profit oriented publishing scenario grabbed this opportunity to build the repositories and eventually succeeded in its endeavor. With the mandate to bring together and preserve the intellectual output of individual institutions many universities came forward to experiment this new flame. In these experiments, unlike the traditional expectations of resistance from the publishing monopolies, the strong resistance came from within the institution's faculties, mainly because of its inexperience with the open archiving and open access concepts and the further copyright commitments with the publishers. While the academia feared over the uncertainty of intellectual theft, the administrators feared the exposure of their institution's intellectual scarcity. With its initial resistance from the conservatives, slowly the academia learnt the benefits of Open Access and many came forward to publish their works in their institution's servers. This marked the significant success of the Institutional Repository model of scholarly publishing towards creating a world of free and open access scholarly society.

The libraries' role towards build up in Institutional Repositories is articulated as follows (Crow, 2002):

- Academic libraries have the Responsibility for managing and archiving all printed materials in IRs.
- Library program and budgets will have to support faculty open access publishing activities.
- To the organizational imperatives to invest in the future, institutional repositories offer a compelling response.
- Libraries are to provide the document preparation expertise to help authors contribute their research to IRs.

4. CHANGING SCENARIO OF SCHOLARLY COMMUNICATION

There are three models in scholarly communication which the world has generally accepted, viz., and traditional paper based journal publishing process which has a track record of over 300 years. E-publishing on commercial basis and the Open Access mode of publishing. The developments in IT and internet have contributed considerably to shrink the supply chain of information and it is indeed a welcome change. For the information industry, the supply chain extends from the source of information to the point of usage. The traditional journals in paper format took 36-52 weeks for journals to publish. Surprisingly enough, in this total cycle time of 1 year the value addition (generation, review, correction and printing) takes place in not more than 2-3 weeks, indicating a huge wastage of time and money contributed mostly by non value adding links. In this context, the advent of the E-publishing has really been a boost to the scholarly publishing domain, bringing down the publishing time frame to a remarkable 3-4 weeks.

A noticeable departure from the traditional systems here is that the printing is delinked from the publishing process. It is important to note here that the much appreciated and respected scholarly value systems are not compromised even by a single degree in relation to quality checks in the new process. In fact it improves and strengthens them with its inherent advantages of being online with respect to processes and procedures. The third category is the growing sets of open access publishing and scholarly archive initiatives, which are the offshoots of the novel open access movement, catching up globally. Authors are now able to publish their findings at an astoundingly fast pace such as 10-15 minutes or even at a lesser time. The relative features and merits of the three systems are illustrated in the following figure below:-

5. INSTITUTIONAL REPOSITORIES

The Institutional Repositories include all digitized materials like electronic theses and dissertations, journals articles, monographs and other learning objects. It is online archive for the intellectual output of a particular institution for collecting, preserving and disseminating to the research community. It can be viewed as a set of services that institutions offer to members of the academic community to maintain and provide the digitized materials. It provides open access to the institution's research output and may be varied from one another. The set of technical standards ensures that it exposes the metadata of all items in their contents to the open access in the same basic way. It is the harvesting of metadata through the open archives for the intellectual research output. The contents are indexed for the search purposes using many search engines like Google and Google Scholar to create open access databases at the global level. The open access nature will be definitely increasing the scholarly literature for self-archiving.

Institutional repository is the marquee of an institution in the world, where institution displays its worthwhile research programmes, projects, and initiatives to the broad spectrum of audience in the world. An institution outreaches its findings that in turn encourage other institutions and organizations to collaborate and to share their knowledge, expertise and skills. Institutional repositories offer seamless access to documents and reflect past and present research interests of the institution as well as its future research goals. It makes the publications more usable by contemporary and future scholars as well as other professionals like policy makers and social workers. The pace of scholarly communication would be highly accelerated if the IR holds research papers, research reports, etc as soon they are made public.

This also have publications in receiving more citations, since the research findings are quickly available to the fellow scholars. The IR can be used throughout the institution and collaborative institutions. Some institutional repositories in India are only providing access to metadata to the external communities who are accessing their repository through internet, whereas internal members who are accessing their repositories through intranet are getting full text information besides metadata. These restrictions exist due to various reasons involving copyright issues, bandwidth issues, permissions from the grant providing agencies (GPA's), and so on. In India there are number of research grant providing agencies. Sometimes some areas may overlap with each other. Using institutional repositories, the GPA's can evaluate the novelty of a research proposal and come to know whether any study has been already undertaken in a particular area or discipline.

Institutional repositories have been established in academic and research libraries. University based institutional repositories manage, Disseminate and preserve where Appropriate digital materials created by the institution and its community members. They also organize and access these materials, (Lynch, 2003). A survey conducted by the Coalition for Networked Information (CNI) found that research libraries have taken on a leadership role in both policy formulation and operational deployment roles for Institutional Repositories at research Universities.

5.1. Objectives

Following are the objectives of an Institutional Repository:-

- To determine awareness about IR publishing.
- To determine awareness about IR software and open access publishing.
- To know the sources from where users are aware about IR publishing
- To identify the motivating factors for using IR publishing
- To find out strategies to develop and improve the IR publications
- To provide access to institutional research output by self-archiving
- To create global visibility for an institutions scholarly research
- To Preservation of information repository content for perpetual access
- To store and preserve others institution's digital assets

- To collect content in a single location.

E-learning : An instructor wants to store problems for a web based home work system in a repository. The problems themselves are expressed in a markup language that requires external application to render. The instructor would like to be able to efficiently search for problems render appropriately when delivered to students' browsers.

Repository management : Operators of the repositories listed in these use case need to be able to manage these facilities and the content. The repository manager then needs to develop tools to deal with a large-scale format migration. Repositories need to provide reporting facilities and interfaces that will support these activities.

Integration with traditional publishing systems and development personalization of e-information services.

5.2. Characteristics

Gibbons identifies the five core features of an Institutional Repository :

- It is institutionally defined - unlike a subject repository; the Institutional Repository captures only the intellectual output of host institution.
- Content may be purely scholarly, or may comprise administrative, teaching and research materials, both published and unpublished.
- It is cumulative and perpetual. Once item are submitted they should not be withdrawn. This carries with it a long term obligation on the host institution to preserve Institutional Repository content.
- It is open and interoperable- a primary goal of an Institutional Repository is to disseminate the institution's intellectual output.
- In collecting, storing and disseminating information

it contributes to the process of scholarly communication.

5.3. Functions

Gibbons list the six core functions of Institutional Repository:-

- Material submission
- Metadata application
- Access control
- Discovery support
- Distribution
- Preservation

5.4. Contents

An Institutional Repository may contain a variety of material produced by the researchers of the institution like...

- Pre print of articles or research reports submitted for publishing the text of journals articles accepted for publication
- Revised text of published work with comments from academic readers
- Conference papers
- Teaching material
- Student's projects
- Doctoral thesis and dissertations
- Database resulting from research projects
- Committee papers, administrative papers
- Computer software work of art
- Photographs and video recordings

5.5. Benefits

The main primary advantages appear to include:-

(a) For users

a. Expansion of the range of knowledge that can be shared.

b. Opportunities to simplify and extend dissemination.

(b) For institution

a. Enabling of intellectual property rights to be exploited more effectively at institution level.

b. Leverage of existing investment in information and content management systems.

c. The highlighting of the quality of intellectual capital.

(c) For all

Opportunities of new forms of scholarly communication.

Flexible way to develop existing scholarly communication.

5.6. Technical Aspects of an Institutional Repository

With regards to technical aspects of institutional repository development, specifically the software and hardware used to run repositories, there is a surfeit of information (McKay 2007).There is a tradition in the literature of repository managers publishing case studies of their institutional repository deployment (Barwick 2007, Bevan 2007) including technical requirements of software, hardware and support. The software user groups peer support through email lists and wikis (DSpace 2008, Eprints 2008).

The general consensus gleaned from the literature is that there are two key software platforms DSpace and Eprints and several other lesser used platforms. Discrimination between the two key platforms tends to be on grounds of preference or existing technical abilities (University of Bath 2008). In addition there are organizations that provide a managed solution based on the open source software for a fee, for example Open Repository (Open Repository 2008) and Digital Commons (Berkley Electronic Press 2008) which can also offer additional related services, for example faculty liaison materials to encourage deposit. These managed services remove or minimize the need for in-house technical expertise when deploying a new institutional repository. This in effect means that the technical aspects of institutional repository development and deployment that dominated the experiences presented in the early literature have now been essentially sidelined, and creating a new repository is, from a technical point of view, reasonably straight forward. This increased ease of implementation is reflected particularly in newer studies looking at institutional repository 'ecology' or "the interactions between repositories and other systems, processes, and people" (Robertson 2008), which is reflected in the focus of this investigation. However, it is worth noting that institutional repositories are regarded as still in their infancy, both as a technology and a resource (A Schenbrenner 2008), and so further changes of both the software and role of the repository is likely in the future, perhaps leading to further specialization of repository functions and fracturing of the definitions of institutional repositories. Information regarding the evaluation of the performance of institutional repositories will therefore be necessary to ensure they are able to achieve the roles and targets set for them.

5.7. Software for Academic Institutional Repository

There are many world renowned open source software used to create repositories are EPrints, DSpace, FEDORA, CDSware etc. They are issued either under GNU public license or the BSD license and can be downloaded from their own sites or open source software directories such as SourceForge. Each of the software has a host of features, unique facilities and excellent capabilities, which the users could explore and experiment.

(i) Greenstone digital library software

The New Zealand Digital library Project at the University of Waikato produces greenstone digital library software. This project is a research program aiming to develop the underlying technology for digital libraries and make it available publicly so that other can use it to create their own collections. The main architects of the software are Roger McNab and Stefan Boddie. Greenstone is a suite of software for building and distributing the digital library collection. It organizes the collection digitally for publishing it on the internet or on CD-ROM. This software is developed and distributed in cooperation with UNESCO and the human info NGO. It is a open source software available from http://www.Greenstone.org under the term of the GNU General public license.

(ii) GNU E-Print Archiving software (Version 2.2.1)

E-Print software is developed as a part of digital library project at University of Southampton, UK. It is available free under the term of GNU General public license. It runs under the Linux and creates online archive libraries of electronic prints. The default configuration creates a research paper archive, but could not be modified and use for other purpose. The document can be stored in any format and each individual research paper (e-print) can be stored in more than one format. The eprint can be submitted through powerful www-based interface. The data integrity checks are performed.

(iii) Prototype E-Prints

Initially, we set up a prototype repository service at the NCSI to facilitate formulation of requirements for the production service and also to address technical issues. The prototype development specifically focused on the following aspects of the repository:

- User interface design
- Document types and document formats to be supported
- Browse views to be created
- Repository policies needed for submission, approval, and copyright and access management
- Creation FAQs for the prospective submitters periodic discussion meetings were also held with the ministry's scientists. This helped us in understanding the needs and requirements of the ministry. Experiences gained from the prototype repository helped us to incorporate the needs and the requirements of the ministry in the production service.

5.8. User interface design

The look and feel of ePrints has been designed as per the specifications of Organization. Several useful features have been taken into consideration while designing the homepage. These include listing of total number of records in the repository as on date, listing of latest records uploaded to the repository, submission guidelines for those who intend to self-archive their publications, FAQs about the repository, guidelines for copyright conformance, provision for depositing articles by email, access to browse views, and links to other repositories that are related to organization.

5.9. Document types and file formats

By default, GNU EPrints supports various document types such as journal articles, conference papers, monographs, books, book sections, etc. The default document types can be customized as per the local needs. As far as the document formats are concerned, the GNU ePrints software does not impose any restrictions on them. It is up to the repository policy as to what file formats are to be allowed or what to be disallowed. And, when it comes to viewing of files, the end-user computer system should have the requisite software to handle the file formats. Here again, GNU Software has nothing to do with the handling of file formats. To render audio and video content, the repository service provider should facilitate streaming of such content. Streaming feature is not directly supported by GNU software. For the present. Both simple and advanced searches are supported by the software. The advanced search facilitates in limiting a search to a specific field.

5.10. Browse views

The browsing functionality facilitates in browsing the records in the repository. For ePrints several browse views have been created. These include browse by authors, document type, year of publication, funding agency, institutions etc., one for the Institution, a programme supported by the Organization and the other by authors.

Subject categories

Categorizing the records that are uploaded in a repository is always a helpful feature. It helps the users to easily locate records pertaining to specific categories. To be able to categorize the records based on a subject classification scheme, the application software should support such functionality. GNU EPrints supports in implementing a subject.

Copyright compliance

Ideally, an IR should hold the final accepted versions of all publications produced in an institute. In reality, this does not happen. If it has to happen then the institutes and the funding agencies will have to mandate open access.

OAI compliance and interoperability

GNU EPrints is compliant with version 2.0 Open Access Initiative Protocol for Metadata Harvesting (OAI-

PMH). This functionality is referred to as OAI compliance. OAI-PMH provides an application in dependent interoperability framework based on metadata harvesting[6]. OAI-PMH defines a mechanism for harvesting records containing metadata from OAI compliant repositories.

DSpace

DSpace is a platform that allows you to capture items in any format – in text, video, audio, and data. It distributes it over the web. It indexes your work, so users can search and retrieve your items. It preserves your digital work over the long term. DSpace provides a way to manage your research materials and publications in a professionally maintained repository to give them greater visibility and accessibility over time. DSpace is typically used in an institutional repository.

It has two main roles :

- Facilitate the capture and ingest of materials, including metadata about the materials
- Facilitate easy access to the materials, both by listing and searching

Benefits of using D-Space

- Getting your research results out quickly, to a worldwide audience
- Reaching a worldwide audience through exposure to search engines such as Google
- Storing reusable teaching materials that you can use with course management systems
- Archiving and distributing material you would currently put on your personal website
- Storing examples of students' projects (with the students' permission)
- Showcasing students' theses (again with permission)
- Keeping track of your own publications/bibliography

- Having a persistent network identifier for your works, that never changes or breaks
- No more page charges for images. You can point to your images persistent identifiers in your published articles.

6. CONCLUSION

Institutional Repositories represent the logical convergence of faculty-driven self-archiving initiatives, library dissatisfaction with the monopolistic effects of the traditional and still-pervasive journal publishing system, and availability of digital networks and publishing technologies. As Institutional Repositories are the face index of any Institute or University shows the status of its strength in the form of research productivity and as such importance be given for development of Institutional Repositories, for which Libraries needs to take positive initiation to develop the scientific temper of the institution.

REFERENCES

1. Coyle K (2006). Mass digitization of books. Journal of Academic Librarianship: 32(6): 41–5. Crow, R. (2002). The Case for Institutional Repositories: A SPARC Position Paper Scholarly Publishing and Academic Resources Coalition, Washington, DC, available at: www.arl.org/sparc/IR/IR_Final_Release_102.pdf.
2. Coyle K (2006). Mass digitization of books. Journal of Academic Librarianship: 32(6): 41–5.
3. Crow, R. (2002). The Case for Institutional Repositories: A SPARC Position Paper Scholarly Publishing and Academic Resources Coalition, Washington, DC, available at: www.arl.org/sparc/IR/IR_Final_Release_102.Pdf
4. Crow, J. (2008). Open access and scholarly communication SPARC/ Science commons. http://ar.org/Sparc. (Retrieved on 19-10-2009).
5. Drak, Miriam A (2004). Institutional Repositories: Hidden Treasures. Searcher, 12(5), 2004.
6. Lynch, C. (2004), "An interview", RLG DigiNews, Available at www.rlg.org/en/ page.php?Page_ID=19481, 8(4)

(Accessed on 11th May 2000 Walter, Tyler. O (2006). Strategies and framework for institutional repositories and the new support infrastructure for scholarly communication. Z)-£/6 A/b^az/«e, 12(10), 121.

7. Farriera, Miguel (2008). Carrots and sticks: some ideas on how to create a successful Institutional repository. D-Lib Magazine, 14(1/2).

8. Karmakar, Gaurishankar (2010). Institutional repositories in India: A comparative study of Dspace and Eprints. Retrieved from http://iam.inflibnet.ac.in:8080/dxml/bitstream/handle/1 944/43 .pdf? Sequence

9. Mittal, Rekha and Mahesh, G (2008). Digital repositories in India: An evaluative study, Electronic Library and information systems, 42(3), 286.

10. Jain, Sanjeev Kumar and Shrivastava, Anurag (2008). Op.cit.p.147.Das, Anup Kumar, Sen, B K and Dutta, Chaitali (2005).op.cit.p.224.

PART-VI
Legal and Language Issues in ICT

13
Copyright Issues in the Digital Environment

Dr. Nasirudheen.T

1. INTRODUCTION

Copyright is an exclusive right of producers, authors, creators, compilers etc... granted by law by the concerned authorities. These rights provide the copyright owner the protection for a limited period of time over the use of his/her works like their reproduction and distribution. The creator of a work can prohibit or authorize its reproduction in various forms, including printing, recording, broadcasting, public performance translation or adaptation.

There are two theories behind copyright, 1. economic protection theory and 2. moral argument theory. The economic protection theory says that, creativity in society is a good thing. In order to encourage creativity, the creator needs incentives. Such incentive includes providing

* Junior Librarian, University of Calicut, Kerala.

limited monopolies with an economic value, such that the author can sell or dispose of his creation for monitory benefit. The moral rights theory argues that, there is an intangible relation between a creator and creation and this relationship remains even after the sale of creation.

2. COPYRIGHT ACT OF INDIA

Copyright act was passed in India in 1914. It was more or less same to the British copyright act 1911, except some modification to the Indian context. The present copyright act was passed in 1957. The Copyright Act, 1957 came into effect from January 1958. Indian copyright Act has been amended six times. (1983, 1984, 1992, 1994, 1999 and 2012). The last amendments, in 2012 is the most significant one especially in this ICT era.

The statutory definition of copyright in India vide section 14 of the copyright act, 1957(Government of India. Ministry of Law and justice,1957). is, "right to do or authorize others to do certain acts in respect of

(a) literary, dramatic or musical works.

(b) Artistic work

(c) Cinematographic film, and

(d) Sound recording".

3. DIGITIZATION OF RESOURCES

There are two remarkable inventions in the history of mankind. The first one among these is the invention of wheel which enabled us to travel from one place to another place. The second one is the inventions of computer, Internet and communication technology, which helped us to bring the whole world in to our hands. This has affected each and every spheres of human life. Library and information field is not an exception.

Digitization of resources enables to break the obstacles of space and time. It can be called as library beyond the walls. It means web-based library services provided via the web. This service make the conventional library services available to the irrespective of their time and space. Definitely it will increase the usage of libraries. (Madhusudanan and Nagabhushanan, 2001). According to Arora (2001), web based library services are the technology based modified services of libraries which helps to increase the usage of library in the Internet era.

The benefit of web based services have been discussed in a paper by Ahmed and Pathak. They opined that "library users value the services that they access from their desktops because the web-based library services save lot of time and traveling cost". (Ahmed, 2007; Pathak et al., 2011). The importance of outlook of webportals has been identified by Kanamadi and Kumbar. Their paper opined that library portals should be attractive and informative. It is the representation of library in the we world. Library websites and portals are the synonym of library collection which reflects the strengths and weaknesses of the libraries very effectively. (Kanamadi and Kumbar, 2006).

Ganeshan and Pandian opined that, starting the web based service is not an end, by starting the web based services, library is not supposed to stop the conventional services. (Ganesan and Pandian, 2004).

4. INDIAN COPYRIGHT LAW VERSUS DIGITIZATION

It is a common belief among LIS professionals is copyright laws are against the digitization of documents whether it libraries or other institutes. There are a lot of papers and articles focusing on this issue.

Here the author has tried to prove Indian copyright law is not an hindrance to libraries and other academic community. Here the author put forward three solid evidences regarding this.

1. Indian copyright act 2012 amendment- in the page No.11, Point No. 32 gives an explanation to the "fair deal". It says that " the storing of any work in any

medium by electronic means by a non-·commercial *public library*, for *preservation* if the library already possesses a non- digital copy of the work".(Indian copyright Law, Amendments,2012, Page No. 11).

2. Right To Information (RTI) reply dated 03.11.2014 from the Copyright Board to Mr. Nasirudheen.T regarding the issue of digitization of library resources in Arabic department, University of Calicut, Kerala says that " Storing of any work in any electronic medium for the purposes mentioned in the clause, including the incidental storage of any computer programme which is not itself an infringing copy for the said purposes, shall not constitute infringement of copyright. (Government of India. Ministry of Law and justice, 2012).

3. Judgment of Delhi High court in the case (CS(OS) 2439/2012, I.As. No. 14632/2012 (of the plaintiffs u/O 39 R-1&2 CPC), 430/2013 (of D-2 u/O 39 R-4 CPC) & 3455/2013 (of D-3 u/O 39 R-4 CPC)). The petition was given by five leading publishers namely i) (Oxford University Press, ii) Cambridge University Press, United Kingdom (UK), iii) Cambridge University Press India Pvt. Ltd., iv) Taylor & Francis Group, U.K. and,

The court declined the arguments of complainants and declared that it is not the infringement of copyright law of India. In the 79th page of the judgment says that " copyright is intended to increase and not to impede the harvest of knowledge. It is intended to motivate the creativity of authors and inventors in order to benefit the public.

The bench of Justice Rajiv Shai Endlaw further added in the page No. 85 that " when modern technology is available for comfort, it would be unfair to say that the students should not avail thereof and continue to study as in ancient era. No law can be interpreted so as to result in any regression of the evolvement of human being for the better. (Delhi High court ,2016).

5. CONCLUSION

Based on the above three arguments, it can be clearly stated that digitization of resources kept in libraries in not considered the copyright infringement. Academic and LIS community consider copy right law as an enemy in the world of knowledge communication. Now let us go ahead with the ICT developments and its maximum utilization for the user community.

REFERENCES

1. Ahmed, T. (2007). Networked e-information services to support the e-learning process at UAE University. *The Electronic Library*, 25(3), 349-62.
2. Arora, J. (2001), Web-based digital resources and services: trends and innovations, available at: http://ir.inflibnet.ac.in/bitstream/1944/105/1/cali_24.pdf.
3. Ganesan, P. and Pandian, N.M. (2004). *Evaluating web resources, services and user attitude towards web-based information services at university of Hyderabad library – a study (* Doctoral thesis, University of Hyderbad) available at: *http://shodhganga.inflibnet.ac.in/bitstream/10603/127233/6/chapter%202.pdf.*
4. Kanamadi, S. and Kumbar, B.D. (2006), Web-based services expected from libraries: a case study of management institutes in Mumbai City. *Webology*, available at: www.webology. ir/2006/v3n2/a26.html26.pdf.
5. Madhusudanan and Nagabhushanan (2012). Web-based library services in university libraries in India: an analysis of librarians' perspective. *The Electronic Library,* 30 (5), 569-588.
6. Government of India. Ministry of Law and justice. *The copyright (amendment) Act,2012.* New Delhi.
7. Judgment of Delhi High court in the case (CS(OS) 2439/2012, I.As. No. 14632/2012 (of the plaintiffs u/O 39 R-1&2 CPC), 430/2013 (of D-2 u/O 39 R-4 CPC) & 3455/2013 (of D-3 u/O 39 R-4 CPC)) dated 16.09.2016.

14

Measurement of Service Quality and User Satisfaction Levels Through LibQUAL+ Tool : A Review

Simhachalam Terli
Ramesh Randhi

1. INTRODUCTION

The function of the library is to serve its users" -

* Assistant Librarian,Dr.B.R.Ambedkar Central Library, Adikavi Nannaya University, Rajamahendravaram, Andhra Pradesh.

** Assistant Professor, Department of Library Science, RGUKT, (IIIT), Srikulam, A.P

Samuei Swett Green.

Assessment of university library services should be considered as a management tool, purposely applied to determine how library is serving the needs and expectations of its users effectively and efficiently. As well as identifying the strengths and weakness of its services in order to recommend ways of sustaining and improving the quality of service delivery in an institution. The extent to which library service quality are assess depends on the availability of information resources (both printed & electronic), services rendered, and facilities utilization by the university library users. The currency and relevancy of the information resources properly arrange on shelves, the usefulness of its catalogs and finding tools in providing access to its collection, the ability and cooperation of the library staff to use the facilities available in bringing these information resources and services to the attention of the users, the attitude of the staff in rendering services, are some of the requirements necessary for measuring service quality.

Satisfying users' needs in the university libraries has been the primary objective of both the libraries and the librarians. Users come to library with different needs and expectations. The unfriendly treatment from library staff towards users, the abundance of resources available, and the difficulty in being able to identify these resources also create problems for users. The inability to easily identify the specific use of a library's services because of the new technologies, inadequate and non-functioning of some library facilities, and the difficulty to access information sources can all contribute to user dissatisfaction among university library users

With the advancement of the library service evaluation process, various tools have been devised for evaluation. One of these tools is the development of the "LibQUAL+™". The present study aimed how to evaluate the quality library services provided to the users with the help of LibQUAL+™ Tool. Librarians use this model to the satisfaction level and the gap between gap between user expectations and actual service provided and service quality provided by the library. This tool helps the library to evaluate, improve library services, and change organizational culture and to measure the satisfaction of clients Examined.

2. QUALITY CONCEPT

Quality is an attribute, a characteristic or a trait or an excellence, the possession of which invests a thing, a person or an idea with a sense of superiority1. Prior to assessment of service quality, it would be quite appropriate to know about the inherent characteristics of the quality as described below:

Intangible : Quality like value is imperceptible only when it manifests itself in a person, a matter, a method, or an idea that it is describable.

Relative/Associative : There is nothing like "absolute" quality. Quality is associated with time, place, environment and the people. A quality product or a quality service in one milieu or environment may not necessarily be a quality product or a quality service in another. Similarly, one cannot impose one's own notion of quality on others.

Tendency to Deteriorate : Quality has a natural tendency to deteriorate with the passage of time, shift in environment, and change of values. It is highly perceptible to the facet of obsolescence. Standards are therefore evolved not only to maintain the quality, but also to revise it from time-to-time to further improve it.

Dialectical Relationship between Quality and Quantity : Much is made of the fact that quality tends to go down as the quantity goes up. There is an element of truth in it. But one should not allow oneself to be overwhelmed by this notion and let the quality suffer under the onslaught of quantity. The managerial quality lies in keeping quality abreast of quantity, certainly not behind it and eventually creating conditions in which quantity can troublesome itself into quality. The relationship between the two is of dialectical nature and not of perpetual antipathy.

Quality is a Seamless Whole : Quality is indivisible. It cannot partly 'be' and partly 'not be'. Either it is or it is not. Also, it should not be judged in parts.

Gravin discussed five approaches to define quality:

(a) *Transcendent-based quality* : It is synonymous with innate excellence. Customers usually presume expensive products means high quality or high grade.

(b) *Product-based quality* : The product-based approach views quality as a precise and measurable variable.

(c) *Manufacturing-based quality* : In this approach the focus is on the supply side and is concerned primarily with engineering and manufacturing facilities.

(d) *Value-based quality* : It defines products in terms of cost and prices.

(e) *User-based quality* : According to this approach the goods that best satisfy customer preferences are believed to be of high quality. This approach equates quality with maximum satisfaction.

Gravin provides the following eight quality dimensions that he feels make up quality:

- *Performance* : This refers to how efficient a product is in achieving its intended purpose.
- *Features* : These are elements that supplement a product's basic performance such as cruise control on a car.
- *Reliability* : This refers to how a product performs consistently over its life-cycle.

- *Conformance* : This means that a product must meet or conform with the specifications for its use.
- *Durability* : The degree to which a products stands stress without failure.
- *Serviceability* : The ease to which a product can be repaired.
- *Aesthetics* : The sensory characteristics of a product such as how it looks or how it sounds.
- *Perceived quality* : This is based upon customer perceptions and opinions.

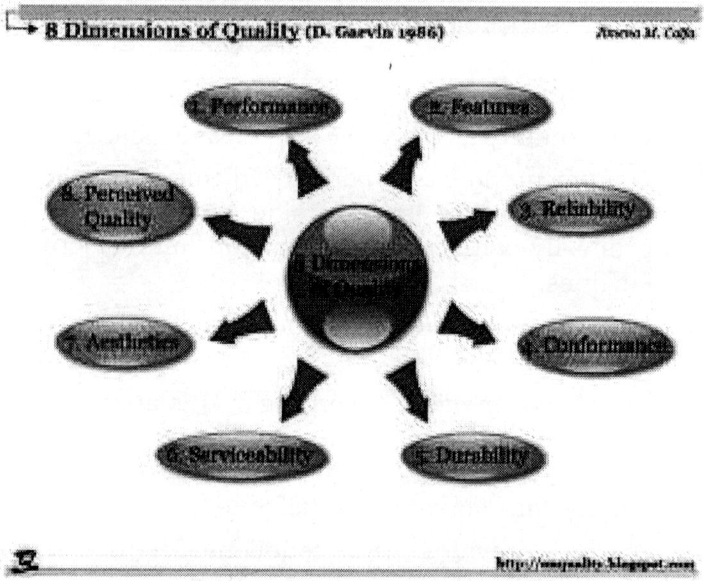

As few products can claim to rank high on all eight dimensions at all times, it is clear that some dimensions can be achieved only at the expense of the other dimensions. Gravin's approaches to quality are largely based on goods. In contrast, Calvert and Hernon focused their studies on service quality and proposed four perspectives of service quality as excellence, value, conformance to specifications, and meeting and/or exceeding expectations. Their research emphasized "meeting and/or exceeding expectations" and led them to develop a framework for service quality in academic libraries.

To achieve high quality in their products and services is essential not only for commercial firms, but also for all non-commercial institutions. Quality will have a different aspect in every institution, but there is a broad consensus in management literature. A short definition that has achieved acceptance is quality is customer satisfaction. "Fitness for use" is an alternate short definition. Unfolding the definition starts with defining the word "customer". A customer is anyone who is impacted by the product or process. A "product" is the output of any process.

In the ISO 9000 standard quality is described as the consistent conformance of a product or service to a given set of standards or expectations. In most definitions quality is defined in relation to the customer or user: "... the key issue is that quality becomes a meaningful concept only when it is indissolubly linked to the aim of total customer satisfaction". Quality of a product or service defined in relation to the customer must not necessarily mean the highest grade possible. A product of a simpler grade may have high quality because it meets the needs and expectations of its target customer group. Quality for one customer or customer group does not always mean quality for another customer or group.

3. SERVICE QUALITY

Service quality is defined in different ways but for the concept of service quality that is used for library evaluation to examine the difference between a user's expectations and the user's perceived sense to actual performance Calvert, (2001). Hernon and Calvert, (1996) also mentioned that most typically, service quality is defined in terms of reducing the gap between user expectations and actual service provided. Though there is ambiguity between the concept of service quality and satisfaction, Hernon (2002) concluded that service quality focuses on the interaction between customers and service providers, and the gap or difference between expectations about service provision and perception about how the service was actually provided. Satisfaction, on the other hand, does not involve gap analysis. Library service quality (LibQual) model is one of the tools that libraries use to solicit, track, understand, and act upon users' opinions of service quality rendered. The three dimensions of service quality measured by Libqual are: affect of service, information control, and library as a place (LibQUAL, 2015). The researcher adapt this model and modify it to suit our local environment through the use of information resources, services rendered, and library facilities available in the university library.

According to library professionals, some librarians think that they can decide the quality of the library service for their users, thinking that they know their users' needs. They also think that users cannot judge the quality of service; users do not know what they want, what would be more useful to them (Kulkarni & Deshpande, 2012). However, such opinions are irrelevant because the only criterion that counts in evaluating service quality is defined by users. Only users judge quality; all other judgments are essentially irrelevant because the users are the most important stakeholders (Parasuraman A. et al, 1985). Without users the library is just a 'warehouse' of information. The users are the ultimate consumers of the library services. The library's success should be measured not in terms of what it has (inputs) but of what it does, the activities it supports, its outputs for example circulation transactions, reference questions answered, classes taught and students enrolled. This also explains the significant role of the library staff, as they have to treat the users as important guests and in that way they will contribute to their satisfaction.

4. SCOPE OF QUALITY ASSESSMENT STUDY IN LIBRARIES

Library quality can have many aspects, and these aspects can change if seen from the point of view of the various stakeholders (are all groups that have an interest in functioning of an institution): for a library the different stakeholders are:

The users (actual and potential). *The function of the library is to serve its users"*

- Samuei Swett Green
- Funding institutions (a university, a community).
- Policy makers.
- Library staff.
- Library Managers
- General Public

5. QUALITY OF INFORMATION SERVICES

Libraries are an important part of higher education institutions, for this reason they do not exist by themselves, but rather to promote institutional missions, usually regarding the development and production of knowledge in teaching, research, and extension and innovation activities. In India, in the educational area, regulating agencies demand a strict quality control to ensure that educational institutions can be accredited or to remain in operation. As part of the infrastructure of these institutions, libraries must evaluate their services.

One of the mechanisms for evaluating higher education in India is the UGC (University Grants Commission), *NAAC (National Academic Accreditation Council), AICTE (All India Council for Technical Education), MCI (Medical Council of India), PCI(Pharmacy Council of India)* created by Ministry of Human Resources Development, GOI by the Law to encourage self-evaluation, accountability, autonomy and innovations in higher education , to collaborate with other stakeholders of higher education for quality evaluation, promotion and sustenance and also to stimulate the academic environment for promotion of quality of teaching-learning and research in higher education institutions in India

Especially, the self-assessment brings to the libraries the opportunity of defining the tool that best captures the perception of their academic community towards their services; however, reports of these experiences were not identified in the Brazilian literature in the area of Library and Information Science, which leads to believe that the own CPA of the universities have been in charge of these evaluations.

The quality of information services should aim the improvement of its services in order to meet or even surpass customers' expectations. For Hernon and Altman (1995 it does not matter what information professionals think about the quality level of their services and as much as some of them may consider that their customers are not capable of evaluating the information services properly, and consider very poorly their opinions, "[...] if customers say there is quality service, then there is".

The same reasoning is followed by Vergueiro, who states that many professionals do not realize the inadequacy of their working practices, imagining that they are offering their best in the circumstances to which they are subjected but they forget that there is another point of view besides the professional - the customer's -, and this mismatch of perceptions may generate a level of service below the satisfactory, compromising its quality. For this reason, a tool that can listen to the customer needs in order to improve the quality of information services is necessary. This is where the evaluation comes to hand.

More than evaluating services, the library professional must have a less systematic overview of his work, that is, a more open approach to the market, including the customers in the evaluation process and, from this point on, considering them the last judges of the excellence of the services. After all, the relationship with customers is the most important aspect of the activities of the information professional.

This prerogative is not new. In the 1930s, Ranganathan advocated the importance of customers to the library services in his laws of Librarianship: the books are for use; every reader his (or her) book; every book its reader; save the time of the reader; the library is a growing organism. Vergueiro sees the contribution of these laws there are contributions to aspects of library service quality and Lancaster, to aspects of evaluation.

Vergueiro has found in the Ranganathan's laws the expression of elements that have been approached by quality theorists, such as the product information professionals work with, the importance of the customer and the search for the satisfaction of their needs efficiently, the need to define work processes that save time for that customer, as well as the understanding that the information services are dynamic and growing organisms.

On his turn, Lancaster identifies in the Ranganathan's laws aspects to be considered in the evaluation processes:

1st Law : focus on accessibility-"[...] can the service make an item accessible to a requester, at the time he or she needs it, from whatever source, in whatever acceptable form?";

2nd Law : focus on availability- "[...] it is not enough that the library owns the book wanted for a user; It is not enough that an item sought by a user is owned by the library; it must also be available when needed";

3rd Law : focus on dissemination-"[...] a library should therefore be evaluated in the terms of its ability to inform people of the materials of potential use to them";

4th Law : focus on efficiency- it must consider the value of the time spent by the customer, i.e. "[...] in the cost-effectiveness analysis of information services, all costs, including all user costs, must usually be taken into account";

5th Law : focus on adaptation to news conditions: changing social conditions and technological developments, but commonly confused with accumulation of information-materials - "[...] libraries should also be evaluated in terms of the extent to which they are able to capitalize on the capabilities provided by technology".

For Lancaster there are several reasons for a library manager wanting to evaluate the services provided:

(a) to establish a scale to show in what level of the performance the service is currently operating;

(b) simply to justify its existence;

(c) to identify possible causes of failures or inefficiency of the service;

(d) To compare the performance of various libraries or services.

For Lancaster the evaluation of information services can be subjective or objective: "[...] subjective studies based on opinions do not cease to be useful, as it is important to know what people feel in relation to the service" and adds that this type of evaluation can and should be followed by objective, quantifiable criteria and procedures.

In the same direction, Lubisco states that, as the object of evaluation, organizational performance are measured both objectively (by data collected from management reports) as well as in a subjective way (from data on customer satisfaction). For her, these two dimensions are complementary, never excluding elements.

Likewise, the International Federation of Library Associations and Institutions (IFLA), in its International

Guidelines for Performance Measurement in Academic Libraries, considers extremely useful that the indicators be followed by topics obtained by a user satisfaction survey in order to confirm or explain the results.

In this sense, an initiative of the Association of Research Libraries (ARL), has demonstrated to be quite suitable for the evaluation of academic libraries, considering the point of view of their customers: the LibQUAL+® methodology (where Lib, library and QUAL, for quality).

6. PARAMETERS OF QUALITY IN LIBRARY AND INFORMATION SCIENCE

Each subject or object of study has its own set of parameters and the same should be assessed or evaluated in terms of those parameters only. Library and information service too has its own parameters for assessment/ evaluation as illustrated in Table 1.

Table 1. Library quality components and parameter

	Component	*Parameter*
Library	Reading material	• Best document for the largest number at the least cost
		• Right document for the right user at the right time.
		• Every document its user
	Library techniques	• Logical but practical
		• Easy to practice
		• Simple to follow
		• Purposive to the specific library
		• Uniform application
	Library users	• Documents are for user
		• Every user his/her document
		• Save the time of the user
	Library building,	• Functional

furniture and equipments	• Aesthetic • Comfortable
Library environment	• Conducive reading atmosphere
Library Staff	• Academically qualified • Professionally trained • Update with information • Motivated
Library Management	• Having capacity to planning, organizing, staffing, directing, coordinating, reporting, budgeting.
Education and training in the library and information science	• Current • Relevant • Having the potential to develop the skills
Research and development in the library and information science	• Relevant • Productive • Promote self-reliance
Library web-page	• Content • Language • Structure • Design • Navigation • Accessibility
Library association	• The protects and promotes the instances of professionals representative

It is possible to assess library collections, services, and facilities from various vantage points. Adopting an organisational perspective, for instance, librarians might examine issues of extensiveness, efficiency, or effectiveness, perhaps even within a cost framework.

Taking a customer perspective, they might examine service quality or satisfaction. One way of evaluation does not preclude the use of others; rather, each offers different insights and opportunities to engage in planning and improved decision-making. There are various options for assessing the quality of library:

(i) Performance indicators : it measures the effectiveness and cost-efficiency of library services. They produce quantified data and are therefore sometimes called "objective".

(ii) User surveys : measure the perceived quality, users' estimate of library services. They produce qualitative data and have a subjective bias.

(iii) Outcome assessment : tries to prove the value and benefit of libraries for individual users and society.

The standards established by Tannare valid for the general assessment of library quality:

- Knowing the customers' needs.
- Faultless delivery of service.
- Good facilities.
- Reliable equipment.
- Efficient administration.
- Efficient back-up service.
- Feedback loops to build in improvement procedures.

The best way for any library to measure quality is to:

- Assess what its users (or non-users) expect from the services they use (or do not use because of bad experience).
- As the funding institution's opinion about what the library should do and how it should perform to support the institution's goals.

7. LIBQUAL+®'S BACKGROUND: THE SERVQUAL METHOD

The first specific model for services evaluation in order to capture criteria for quality services evaluation was assigned to Parasuraman, Zeithaml and Berry (1988).

The evaluation criteria created by these authors take into account the gaps, or rather, the differences between users' expectations and what is actually offered to them. They have considered these gaps as major obstacles in trying to achieve a level of excellence in services provision.

With their study of Gaps, Parasuraman, Zeithaml and Berry (1985) had already given an important contribution to the area. However, as the model did not offer any tool that could measure service quality, the same researchers created in 1988 a scale - that they called SERVQUAL -, in order to analyze qualitative and quantitatively the degree of customer satisfaction in relation towards the offered services

According to Parasuraman, Zeithaml and Berry (1988), customers evaluate service quality comparing what they want and/or expect with what they get. The method points out five dimensions of quality service, as shown in the below Figure 1.

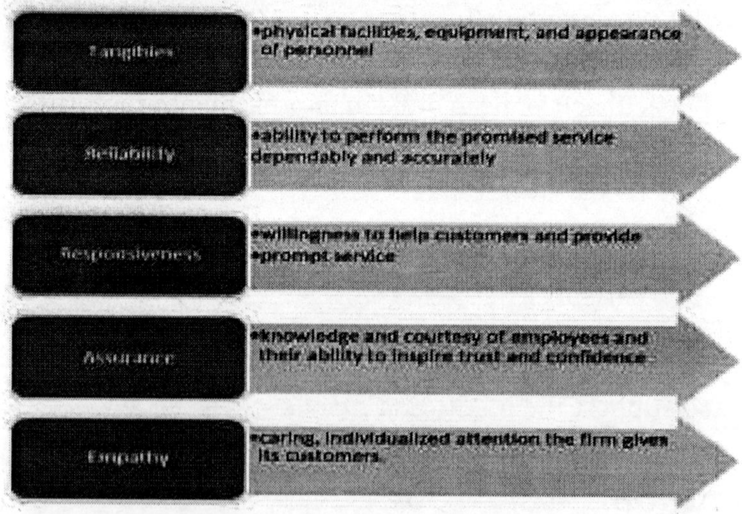

Fig. 1. Dimensions of Parasuraman, Zeithaml and Berry.

The instrument was originally designed by its creators as a questionnaire with twenty-two assertions prepared and distributed among the five dimensions of quality of SERVQUAL method. These assertions are intended to evaluate aspects of quality in relation to customers' expectations and perceptions, from a Likert scale, enabling the calculation of gaps.

At first moment, SERVQUAL was applied to five categories of service: maintenance and repair of household equipment, retail banking, long distance telephony, insurance brokerage and credit cards. However, the authors state that the instrument was designed to be applicable to a variety of services (LOURES, 2009). It can be said that the SERVQUAL method has represented a break in the process of evaluating services and spurred a large number of studies in the area, and many other surveys have refined the conceptual model of Parasuraman and his partners.

SERVQUAL had applications in libraries, with emphasis on the studies of Cook and Thompson (2000), reporting the application in libraries of University of Texas A&M in 1995, 1997, 1999, Sahu (2007) on the application in the library of the Jawaharlal Nehru University (India), as well as Nejati and Nejati (2008), in the library of the University of Tehran (Iran).

Studies on SERVQUAL in libraries admit that the methodology helps breaking the merely professional vision of the service, creating bonds with customers and decreasing the distance between them and the service management, contributing significantly to services management, especially for decision-making and services development. However, the methodology also presents disadvantages, such as: having the data collection instrument composed only by closed questions; not allowing customers to express their opinions, criticisms and suggestions; limiting the research to quantitative data; needing some kind of adjustments regarding the terminology used in the instrument – as, for example, replacing the word 'expectation' for 'importance' and the term 'perception' for 'satisfaction'.

8. WHAT IS LIBQUAL+®

LibQUAL+ is a tool that libraries use to solicit, track, understand, and act upon users' opinions of service quality. The protocol is a rigorously tested web survey that helps libraries assess and improve library services, change organizational culture, and market the library.

The LibQual+®Method

The specific evaluation tool for use in libraries, called LibQUAL+® - Lib (library) and QUAL (quality) - has its history closely linked to the evaluations experiences developed by Texas A&M University (TAMU) using the SERVQUAL methodology.

After three consecutive applications of SERVQUAL in the libraries of TAMU, in 1995, 1997 and 1999, Fred Heath and Colleen Cook, then members of the dean of the libraries' office, concluded that the methodology developed by their university colleagues, professors Parasuraman, Zeithaml and Berry, were heavily focused on the commercial and profitable sector and included items considered irrelevant by library customers, such as the question about library staff costumer.

For this reason, in 1999 Cook, then a PhD student, with one of her professors of statistics in TAMU, Bruce Thompson, requested assistance in developing a specific method for libraries evaluation starting from SERVQUAL. Afterwards, the three researchers, Cook, Thompson and Heath - at that time, members of ARL Council - offered the evaluation method they have developed named LibQUAL to ARL as part of the ARL Program Statistics and Evaluation (ARL's New Initiative Measure2) for non-profit use and libraries improvement.

In spring 2000, with the support of the US Department of Education Fund for the Improvement of the Post-Secondary Education (FIPSE) Grant, the LibQUAL+® was applied to a group of 13 libraries associates to ARL, having inaugurated one evaluation program based on web that would happen, from then on, in an annual basis.

It is possible to say that LibQUAL+® was developed to satisfy the need to perform a research within libraries in order to compare and evaluate their services for benchmarking and identification of best practices purposes.

LibQUAL+® aims to:

- Foster a culture of excellence in providing library service;
- Help libraries better understand user perceptions of library service quality;
- Collect and interpret library user feedback systematically over time
- Provide libraries with comparable assessment information from peer institutions;
- Identify best practices in library service; and
- Enhance library staff members' analytical skills for interpreting and acting on data.

As time goes by, due to an extensive use by libraries around the world, the LibQUAL+® has been revised and improved. In its current version, the instrument contains 22 questions with a free comments field and demographic questions. The survey also contains five additional questions related to information literacy, three questions for satisfaction in general and three more questions about the use of libraries and search portals. Optionally, the library can choose five questions from a database with about 120 questions for additional research. If this option is chosen, these five questions are added to the main part of the survey, comprising then, 27 questions. Since 2010, the LibQUAL+® has a Lite version, which is actually a stripped-down version of the original instrument. In LibQUAL+® Lite, the customer must answer only eight of the 22 questions of the instrument. This selection is made randomly by the system and aims to optimize the time of the respondent (from nine minutes for the 22 questions version to five minutes in the Lite version). Either way, the library will have at the end of the process, the answers for of all 22 questions.

ARL allows the use of the LibQUAL+® by the payment of a fee that guarantees to the associate the access to the system to configure and administer the survey, collect and track the responses. After research completion, the final summary of the data access remains at the library's disposal: information on representativeness, the raw data files in CSV format, the SPSS syntax file, the comments from the survey, and the 'Results Notebook' containing the analysis of the survey results. Registration also gives access to the summary of the data and the 'Results Notebook' of all institutions that conducted research using the LibQUAL+® in the given year, enabling the benchmarking with other institutions. Currently, the rates are around $ 5,500 comprehending registration, annual fee and training.

LibQUAL+® methodology currently has several manuals, tutorials available on its Web site. Following, the procedures will be briefly presented. Developed from a SERVQUAL adaptation for use in libraries, based on statistical studies it reduced the five SERVQUAL dimensions to just three, and then renamed them in order to meet the needs of library service quality evaluation: the Affect of service; Information Control, and Library as place, as shown LIBQUAL+®' dimensions of service.

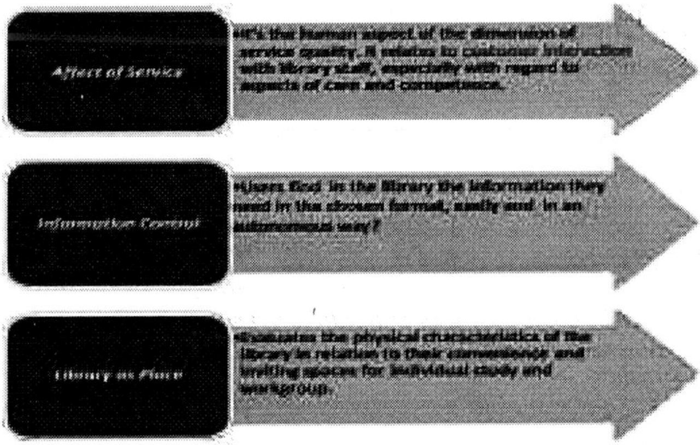

The LibQUAL+® instrument uses a standard methodology for data collection and analysis based on the theory of gaps, where respondents must assign each of the 22 issues a score on a nine-point scale from three perspectives: the minimum level of service; the desired level of service; the observed or perceived level of service, as shown LIBQUAL+® instrument detail.

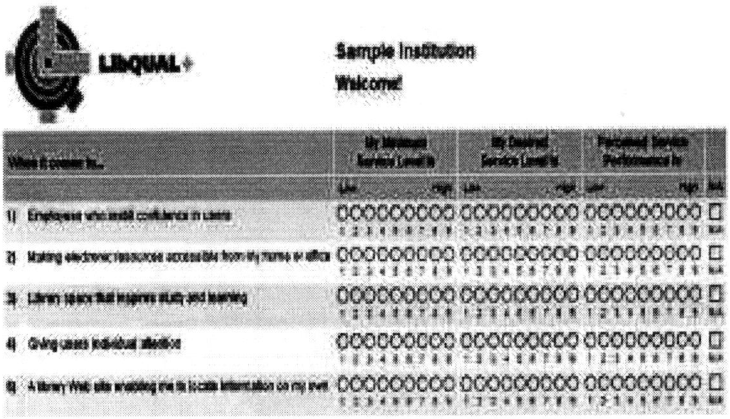

There are two services gap scores on LibQUAL+®. A quality service must have the perception score somewhere between the minimum level of service at the lowest end of the scale and the desired level of service at the higher end. The three scores assigned to a question of the instrument displayed as points on a line. The gap between the minimum level and the desired level defines what the methodology establishes as zone of tolerance.

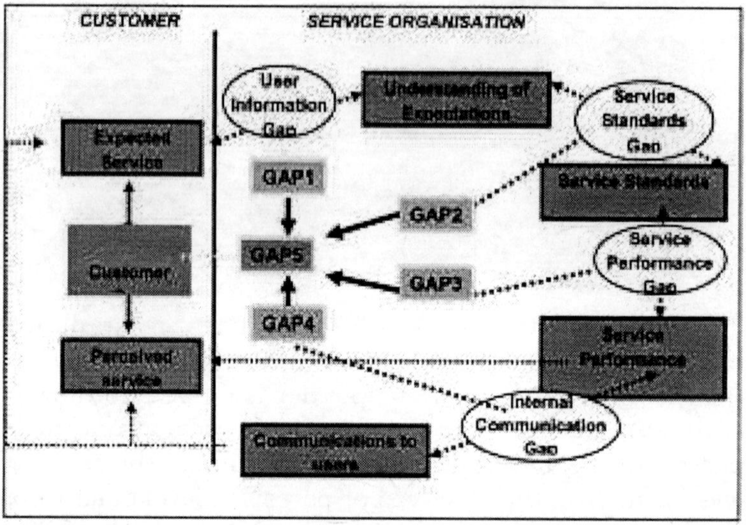

9. HOW WILL LIBQUAL+ IS BENEFIT TO YOUR LIBRARY

Library administrators have successfully used LibQUAL+ survey data to identify best practices, analyze deficits, and effectively allocate resources. Benefits to participating institutions include:

- Institutional data and reports that enable you to assess whether your library services are meeting user expectations
- Aggregate data and reports that allow you to compare your library's performance with that of peer institutions
- Workshops designed specifically for LibQUAL+ participants
- Access to an online library of LibQUAL+ research articles
- The opportunity to become part of a community

interested in developing excellence in library services

10. CONCLUSION

Considering the reality of the academic libraries, LibQUAL+®, will contribute to a more professional administration, providing an appropriate tool for planning and decision-making. In addition, the methodology introduces convergences with other management practices, as well as quality, and assists in the establishment of a knowledge basis on customers and services. If well managed, it will ensure an environment of wide circulation and dissemination of knowledge, the spreading of creativity and the creation of new ideas and learning from the past, consolidating the knowledge management, and optimizing the librarians' time, who, besides the management, also have to deal with the technical and service activities of the libraries.

Another aspect must also be considered: LibQUAL+® implementation brings the library closer to the customers, creating the opportunity to enhance and improve the status of the library in the community it serves and also helping it in obtaining more economic resources for the library. Once adopted by other libraries, the method allows performance comparisons, enabling the identification of best practices, including the establishment of a library ranking, as well as the creation of a national library statistics database, making it possible to compare statistical data on local, national, and inter-institutional levels.

REFERENCES

1. Abbot, C. 1994. Performance measurement in library and information services. London: Aslib.
2. Abubakar, B. M. (2011). Academic Libraries in Nigeria in the 21st Century. *Library Philosophy and Practice*, 1-5.
3. Aguolu, C.C. & Aguolu, I.E. (2002) Libraries and Information Management in Nigeria. Maiduguri; Ed-Linform Services.

4. Aina, I. (2004). *Library and Information Science text for Africa.* Ibadan: the World Information Services Ltd.

5. Akpan-Atata, E., & Enyene, E. T. (2014). Awareness, Availability, and Utilization of ICT Facilities for Effective Service Delivery in Academic Libraries in Nigeria. *Journal of Research in Education and Society*, *5* (3), 1-10.

6. Aluri, Rao. 1993. Improving reference service: the cae for using a continuous qualityimprovement method. ItQ, Vol.33: 220-221, 232

7. Andaleeb, S.S. and P.L Simmonds. 1998. Explaining user satisfaction with academic libraries: strategic implications. College & Research Libraries, Vol.59, no. 2: 156-167

8. Arnau, R.C., Thompson, R.L., & Cook, C. (2001). Do different response formats change the latent structure of responses?: An empirical investigation using taxonometric analysis. Educational and Psychological Measurement, 61, 23-44.

9. Bello, A. A. (2000). Students' use of an academic library: University of Abuja experience. *Library bulletin: journal of the Nigerian Universities Library System*, 14-20.

10. Boulding, W., A. Kalra, R. Staelin, and V. Zeithaml, V. 1993. A dynamic process model of service quality: from expectations to behavioural intentions. Journal of Marketing Research, Vol. 30, no. 1: 7-27

11. Brady, M.K., J.J. Cronin, and R.R Brand. 2002. Performance only measurement of service quality: a replication and extension. Journal of Business Research, Vol.55, No.1: 17-31

12. Broady-Preston J. and H. Preston. 1999. Demonstrating quality in academic libraries. New Library World, Vol. 100(1148): 124-129

13. Calvert, P. (2001). International variations in measuring customer expectations. *Library Trends*, *19* (4), 1-25.

14. Caruana, A, M.T. Ewing, and B. Ramaseshan. 2000. Assessment of the three-column format SERVQUAL: an experimental approach. Journal of Business Research, Vol. 49: 57-65.

15

English Language Skills to Library Professionals: An Analytical Study

*Veerender Kumar, P.**

1. INTRODUCTION

Modern information in any branch of knowledge is more easily available and accessible only in libraries whether online or offline. Everybody needs to depend on libraries for their studies. Globalization and liberalization has boosted in the overall development of the country. As English plays the role of the only link language it has become part of life for many Indians, which is why many can speak fluent and idiomatic English like native speakers. For the younger generation it has become the

* Assistant Professor in English, Sree Chaitanya Institute of Technological Sciences, Karimnagar, Telangana & Research Scholar (PT), Department of English, Kakatiya University, Warangal, TS

passport to success and prosperity. English has become a link language in the real sense of the term. In India it became the language of communication for the classes and the masses in various areas namely — offices, MNCs, colleges, schools etc. Slowly but surely people have started using English language in every walk of their life. As mentioned above English skills namely - listening, speaking, reading and writing skills have become most important language skills for the librarians to lead their role as a successful librarian.

2. ROLES OF LIBRARIAN IN WORK PLACE

1. Demonstrates initiative
2. Excellent reader
3. Good at communication
4. Problem-solving
5. Proficient with computers

Librarians are also responsible for acquiring, organizing, managing and distributing library resources, and also ensuring that library provision meets the needs of all its users. As librarians are responsible for providing support to academic departments, job vacancies may demand a degree that is relevant to a particular subject area. Librarianship is a people-focused role, requiring individuals to manage learning resources while keeping the library users' needs in mind. Duties vary considerably according to the size of library, but typically include:

- Selecting, developing, cataloguing and classifying library resources.
- Answering readers' enquiries.
- Using library systems and specialist computer applications.
- Management of staff, including recruitment, training and/or supervisory duties.
- Liaising with departmental academic staff, external

organizations and suppliers.

- Ensuring that library services meet the needs of particular groups of users (e.g. staff, postgraduate students, disabled students).
- Managing budgets and resources.
- Supporting independent research and learning.
- Developing IT facilities.
- Assisting readers to use computer equipment, conduct literature searches etc.
- Promoting the library's resources to users.

Depending on where you work, some travel between libraries on different campuses can be necessary. Working hours are generally nine to five from Monday to Friday; however, some services are increasingly open during evenings, weekends and sometimes even on a 24-hour basis. Despite this, there is scope for shared work and flexible working hours.

Most librarians enjoy finding out more about a sector, subject area and helping others with their research areas. Responsibility for specific library functions or subjects is common even in basic level posts, and developing skills and expertise through increasingly specialized or advanced roles will steadily advance career prospects.

3. TYPICAL EMPLOYERS OF ACADEMIC LIBRARIANS

- Universities and their academic departments
- Research institutes
- Public libraries
- Higher and further education colleges
- Professional and learned societies
- Specialist departments within government, hospitals, and large professional firms

4. KEY SKILLS FOR LIBRARY PROFESSIONALS

Employers seek confident individuals with excellent organizational and interpersonal skills. Other key skills include:

- Strong IT skills and familiarity with the use of databases and the Internet.
- Team working and management skills.
- Assessment of resources and library users' needs.
- Presentation and verbal communication skills.
- Subject-specific knowledge or expertise in a particular function, for example ICT resources or resource ordering.

This paper focuses on English language skills which help librarians to execute their duties effectively. They can be elaborated as follows: (a) Librarian should have command on English language only then he can do works likeSelecting, developing, cataloguing and classifying library resources, otherwise he may lose his reputation and job. (b) In order to answer readers' enquiries he should be having sound knowledge of English if not he will have to face many challenges in execution on his duties. Most of the institutions will have students from all over the country who do not communicate in other language except in English. (c) Using library systems and specialist computer applications librarians command over language English comes to rescue him in his job. (d) Librarian will have reputation only when he is good at English to organize Managing staff, including recruitment, training and/or supervisory duties. (e) A librarian's job also includes duties like liaising with departmental staff, external organizations and suppliers in getting his work done. Librarian has to talk to Users regarding the requirement of purchasing books. He also has to speak and write to external organizations and suppliers to procure required materials. Here in the above said area librarian's language skills play a crucial role. (f) Any Librarian has to communicate to ensuring that library services meet the needs of particular groups of users (e.g. staff, users, students, disabled users), hence they must be good in communication skills particularly language skills.

Some more skills academic librarians should possess in executing their job are as follow:

4.1. Administration of library

In maintaining rapport with the students, staff and management a librarian should possess good language and soft skills, otherwise he may fail in management of library.

4.2. ICT and Technological Development of Library Information and Software systems

In acquiring new technologies for the upgrading one's library one should have excellent skills in understanding the developments in this field.

4.3. Reference and Referral Services

To provide users sufficient reference and referral services, a librarian should see that he make everything available. Also a librarian should research developments in the area of interest of users. For that they should have good listening, reading, speaking and writing skills.

4.4. Seminars, Conferences, Workshops etc.

In organizing Seminars to students, staff, and different faculties and even to fellow librarians, a librarian should possess skills like listening, speaking; writing to all the concerned individuals regarding the work and also one should have excellent reading skills to gather required information regarding the work to make the program success.

4.5. Articles and Paper Publications

In order to write articles and research papers one should have good reading, writing and listening skills otherwise the task cannot be achieved. Good knowledge over the above said skills only will make the candidate excel in improving and upgrading qualification and quality of the librarian.

4.6. Research

In order to do successful research in one's area of interest a librarian should acquire good reading, writing, speaking and listening skills.

4.7. House Keeping Operations

To write Circulars, to manage Periodicals, To arrange books in order, to maintain Files and Filings, to do correspondence with required personnel one should have good English language skills.

4.8. Interviews

To grow in one's life one should seek good employment opportunities, for that one should attend as aspirant for better positions. In order to chase one's dream one should possess excellent English language skills and soft skills which are called life skills.

4.9. Receiving Officials and Dealing with higher authorities

One should seize good language skills and soft skills to receive and deal with officials and higher authorities. Then only one can have good reputation and recognition in his work, which also helps in solving users' problems and understanding users' needs.

4.10. Editorial Role

Users also many a time request for editorial services as most of the librarians have vast experience in editorial work, here their language skills pay good prize.

4.11. Reviewer

Most of the librarians because of their extensive

reading habit know how to review books, journals and other write ups, their command over language decides this particular job. Most of the people 'the needy' for reviewing their write ups approach librarians.

4.12. Authorship

Because of their vivid exposure to books most of the librarians grow interest in writing; which again puts the hurdles of language skills particularly English language to make them heard globally. Hence here also English language skills play vital role.

4.13. Online Services

Today every library has online and offline books facilities. To do particularly online communication a librarian should well versed in English language. Otherwise he cannot put forward users' demands and his personal demands to get the required materials available in his library.

4.14. Trouble Shoot

When technical problem arises in maintaining library software a librarian should have to follow according to the instructions of the system which are only in English language. There he needs to have good awareness in reading the commands of the system to perform further. Otherwise a librarian cannot trouble shoot his systems in the library.

4.15. Q & A

In the process of running online and offline services to the users a librarian should communicate maximum only in English. Hence he particularly should have good command over English language skills else he cannot move ahead in his career and in routine also.

5. CONCLUSION

Need of English language skills to a library and

information professional can be understood from the above mentioned article. It is also understood that to maintain and to excel in one's career - a library and information professional has to have very good knowledge over English language then only he will survive in his profession. All the major areas where a Library and Information professional intersects with English language skills in execution of his duties have been identified and discussed in brief account. It is also cleared understood that only by having excellent English language skills only a library professional can lead a good career and have reputation and honor in society.

REFERENCES

1. Anjali Ghanekar, Business Communication Skills, Everest, 2011.
2. Business English Dictionary, Pearson, 2013.
3. David Irwen: Effective Business Communications, Viva-Thorogood, 2013.
4. Leman and Dufrene Sinha, BCOM (Business Communication), 2nd Edition, Cengage, 2012.
5. Lesikar: Basic Business Communication, Tata Mc Grah Hill, 2013.
6. Rajendra Pal, J S Korlahahi: Essentials of Business Communication, Sulthan Chand and Sons, New Delhi, 2013.
7. Sailesh Sengupta, Business and Managerial Communications, PHI, 2011.
8. Sehgal: Business Communication, Excel, 2013.
9. Stephen Bailey, Academic writing for Internal Students of Business, Routledge, 2013.
10. http://www.bbc.co.uk/languages/yoursay/language_and_identity/global_english/english_is_a_link_language.shtml
11. http://shodhganga.inflibnet.ac.in/bitstream/10603/9578/9/09_chapter%201.pdf